Catalysts for Your Prayers

Catalysts for Your Prayers

Over 300 inspired prayer catalysts to activate your prayers to the next level and to reveal in your spirit the deeper things of God.

H. R. Chowdhry

Copyright © 2012 by H. R. Chowdhry.

ISBN:	Softcover	978-1-4691-5499-2
	Ebook	978-1-4691-5500-5

All rights reserved. No part of this book may be reproduced or transmitted in any form or by any means, electronic or mechanical, including photocopying, recording, or by any information storage and retrieval system, without permission in writing from the copyright owner.

This book was printed in the United States of America.

To order additional copies of this book, contact:
Xlibris Corporation
0-800-644-6988
www.xlibrispublishing.co.uk
Orders@xlibrispublishing.co.uk
303397

Contents

Foreword 9
Acknowledgement 11
Introduction 13

Chapter 1: Basics of Prayer 19
   A. What is the true meaning of prayer? 19
   B. What is the necessity and the importance of prayer? ..20
   C. What are the key points to effective prayer? 21
   D. What are the different types of prayers? 22
   E. What is intercession? 23

Chapter 2: Short Prayers of Mixed Categories 26
   A. Praise and adoration to God 26
   B. Thanksgiving to God 28
   C. Dependence on God and calling upon Him for help ..29
   D. Confession to God for the great need to
      live a true Christian life 30
   E. Forgiveness of God to us and our forgiveness to others ..32
   F. Provision of God (for all our needs) 33
   G. Protection of God (in sufferings/temptations/tests) ...35
   H. Church of God 37
   I. Confidence in God and in His promises 38
   J. Hindrance to prayers (unanswered prayers or delay in answer) ...41
   K. Believing and using God's Word 43

Chapter 3: Prayers Concerning Love 47
   A. God's love for us 47
   B. Our love for God 51
   C. Our love for each other 52

Chapter 4: Intercessory Prayers 56
   A. Prayers for the lost (in variety of ways) 56
   B. Prayers for the sick in body, mind, or spirit 57
   C. Prayers for creation and environment 59
   D. Prayers for the nations and their governments 61
   E. Prayers for the Church 63
   F. Prayers for not taking God seriously or rejecting Him 64
   G. Intercessory prayers previously used in Sunday worship 65

Chapter 5: The Conclusive Prayer 79
   Praying through Psalm 23 79

Do you need Prayer Support? 81

Let us then approach the throne of grace with confidence, so that we may receive mercy and find grace to help us in our time of need.

(Hebrews 4: 16)

Foreword

I have known H. R. Chowdhry for well over a decade and during that time we have frequently and regularly studied the Holy Bible and prayed together. I have grown to admire her devotion to the Lord Jesus Christ and her absolute trust in Him.

Here is a book, *Catalysts for Your Prayers*, that gives you a simple and straightforward understanding of the Christian prayer. The book provides a collection of short and helpful prayers to enable you to pray in any situation in which you find yourself—whether to praise the Lord or to give Him thanks, to acknowledge His Lordship over your life, or to call upon Him in your needs. I pray that these simple yet inspirational prayers will lead you to higher level of trust and dependency on Him and will be a great blessing to you.

Maureen Haffner

Acknowledgement

It is amazing how I have witnessed this book; *Catalysts for Your Prayers* take shape and form. I was encouraged to write about 100 prayers by my eldest son Samuel and to share them with others on the Internet. One day I sat and wrote about thirty prayers in one go, most of them were just flowing out, and I was jotting them on paper. As I took serious interest, the Holy Spirit led me one step further every time.

I am neither a writer nor an expert on the subject of prayer, and I am still in the process of learning and studying God's Word. I regularly gain knowledge from sound Bible teaching and keep myself engaged in the activity of prayer.

However, the only qualification I consider to have in writing this book is that I am the recipient of God's grace in Lord Jesus Christ. Unashamedly, I am a disciple of Lord Jesus Christ, and in His Spirit, the Lord Jesus Christ lives in me. Whilst writing this book, the power of the Holy Spirit was sufficiently available to me. Therefore, with all my heart I offer my praise and thanks to the King of power and glory.

The Lord has always been good to me with the provision of prayer partners, but there are some who were extraordinarily faithful and dedicated to prayer. I am thankful to the Lord for Louise Frost (who is with the Lord now) and for Marcel, who joined me in the weekly intercessory prayers in my house in the 1980s. We were regularly blessed with the presence and power of God. Many prayers were answered, and though some prayers seemed to be unanswered, yet we learnt to pray persistently.

I am thankful to the Lord for Hazel Heorder (who is with the Lord now), from whom I received genuine motherly love, care, and support in every way but especially with her prayers for myself and for my family. She was not only a good friend, but also a strong intercessor prayer partner for over twenty-five years; I learnt a lot about the Christian faith with her.

But I thank the Lord that He replaced Hazel with Maureen Haffner, my present prayer partner. We come together to pray every week, and we are learning together how to be effective and faithful intercessors. I am thankful to her for all the encouragement and the support she has given me in the publication of this book on prayers.

This book is dedicated to my grandfather, who converted to Christianity and left the inheritance of the Christian faith for his coming generations. I am thankful to the Lord for my parents who brought me and my sisters up in the Christian faith and disciplined us in reading God's Word and in prayer. I have done the same for my sons, and so I also dedicate this to Samuel and Paul. I am thankful to them because they gave me all the possible support I needed to publish this book. My prayer is that they will grow day by day in their walk with the Lord and glorify the Lord Jesus Christ in everything that takes place in their lives. Amen.

H. R. Chowdhry

Introduction

At very early age I realised the importance of prayer; ever since then I have been learning to pray. My prayer to Lord Jesus Christ was, is, and always will be to teach me to pray, and so I am a lifetime student of the Holy Spirit, though I know that in this life I will never be able to have the full knowledge of how to pray effectively. One way to learn is to take a bold and practical step to start asking the Holy Spirit to pray through you, for you, in you, and with you.

'People ought to pray and not to lose heart' is the teaching of our Lord Jesus Christ. So praying is obedience and pleasing to God, and therefore is it wise on our part to be engaged in this spiritual activity all the time.

What is the aim of *Catalysts for Your Prayers*?

The aim of the book is not to provide an in-depth study on the subject of prayer but to encourage and to support people to get engaged in prayer and to develop their prayer life. Engaging in this brings us closer to God and thus provides opportunities to discover our living God more deeply. Praying also enables us to get a fresh vision of God and to experience His presence and His power. The more we reflect on God's glory and majesty, on His love and grace, on His might and power, the more adoration, worship, praise, and thanksgiving flow out through our prayer.

I felt that it is important to have a basic understanding of prayer. Therefore, the book has provided a small chapter on the basics of prayer, which covers all the aspects of biblical Christian prayer.

The importance of prayer is realised when you count all the spiritual benefits of a prayerful life. It is through this that we can keep our focus on God. A good prayer life establishes and maintains our relationship with God and with others. Our prayers give glory to God; they bless us, sanctify us to make us like Christ, and promote the growth of our faith too. But in the practical aspect of prayer, we all have said similar things like, 'I am not good at putting how I feel into the prayers,' or 'I cannot pray very well,' or 'Praying is hard'. So if the wording and structure of the prayer is becoming a hindrance in your prayer life, please do not be discouraged. Invite the Holy Spirit to pray with you, in you, and for you and to give you the right motives, the right thoughts with the right words to pray. If your heart is right with God and your faith is at work, prayers of silence can be as acceptable as the one using audible words. For this reason I have been prompted by the Holy Spirit to write some prayers. Most of these are spontaneous; there are some which are thoughtfully written, but at the same time they are not perfect and not complete. They are there to further stimulate and to advance your prayers.

Throughout the book there is a strong thread of Christian themes running through the prayers. Most of these are packed and loaded with God's Word. When we pray using God's Word, we are speaking God's mind and His will. It is only the inspired Word of God that gives the subject, the substance, and the backbone to our prayers. Using God's Word for prayer can give us hope, life, courage, strength, peace, and security. It is through His Word that we can learn to depend on God and on His promises. But most importantly, God reveals His will through the Holy Scripture.

This book is for those who have already started their journey of faith in the Lord Jesus Christ, to strengthen the weak in faith, and to grant faith to those who have none.

My desire is that these written prayers will act like catalysts to activate our prayers to the next level and to increase our confidence in God and in His promises. In my spirit, I truly want the prayers that are provided in this book to energise, sustain, and motivate our faith; because without faith it is impossible to please God.

God the Holy Spirit, I put these simple and ordinary prayers under Your influence so that the power of the living Saviour will be awakened through them. I offer my humble efforts in writing these prayers so that something good and beautiful will happen, which has been waiting to take place in our prayer life. Amen.

What does the book provide?

The *Catalysts for Your Prayers* has a chapter titled 'Basics of Prayer', which includes *the true meaning of prayer, the necessity and the importance of prayer, the key points to effective prayer, different types of prayers, and what intercession is.*

The book provides over 300 hundred catalysts of prayer, which fall into three main groups: the prayers of mixed categories, the prayers concerning love, and the prayers of intercession.

The majority of the prayers in this book are of mixed categories, which include *the prayers of adoration and praise, thanksgiving, dependence on God for help, confession to lead a better Christian life, prayers for provision and protection, forgiveness, confidence in God and in His promises, the hindrance to unanswered prayers and delay in answer, Church of God, and believing and using God's Word in prayer.*

I felt the need to write some prayers on the subject of love. Love is the need which all human beings are seeking to receive and make the effort to give. Love is the most prominent theme of the Holy Scripture, and it declares that God is love. God is the source of eternal, pure, self-giving, and intense love. He generously imparts His love into our hearts to enable us to love Him and to love His people.

There are thousands of hymns and songs sung in our worship to God, and lots of sermons have been preached—all based on God's love. Yet many people feel unloved and insecure in the love of God and have lost trust in human love. Through these prayers, my hope is that we will grow in the knowledge of God's love demonstrated in Lord Jesus Christ. I pray that the Holy Spirit will enable us to be obedient and generous to show our love to God and to people in words and in actions.

The prayers concerning love include *the love of God for us, our love for God, and our love for each other.*

The third group is the prayers of intercession; this is one of the greatest services which a Christian can do to God and to His people, and that is to pray to God on the behalf of others.

Intercession is a sacred service which demands no designated position or recognition in the church or in the world but requires great love, care, and concern for the need of hope, life, and change in people and in the world. Our intercession seeks the glory of our risen and ascended Lord. It seeks for His kingdom to come in the lives of people, and His will is to be done on earth as it is done in heaven.

Through Apostle Paul, Lord Jesus Christ is appealing to the Christians everywhere, 'I urge, then, first of all, that requests, prayers, intercession and thanksgiving be made for everyone' (1 Tim. 2: 1).

The intercessory prayers include *the prayers for the lost (in variety of ways); for those sick in body, mind, and spirit; prayers for creation and environment; for the nations and their governments; for the Church; and prayers for not taking God seriously or rejecting God.*

I was led to add seven sets of intercessory prayers as I felt that these prayers are inspired by the Holy Spirit and need to be shared with others. I wrote, prepared, and have used these prayers for the Sunday worship in my own church.

How to use the prayers provided in this book?

God the Holy Spirit is the Lord of these prayers, and He can use them in the way it pleases Him for His purposes and according to our needs. So there are no hard and fast rules on how and when these prayers should be used. These prayers are open and incomplete for you to add the personal details of the situation or to add your specific needs. The prayers are real and living and are provided with the aim that you should make them your own.

I can offer few suggestions, in the hope that it will benefit someone. They are as follows:

- The prayer of adoration, praise, and thanksgiving without a petition is a complete and eternal prayer. A day is coming when we will not ask for our needs because in heaven there will be no lack of anything, no pain, no tears, no struggles, and no sin. The prayer of praise, worship, and thanksgiving will continue to eternity because our eternal Redeemer Lord Jesus Christ is worthy of our worship, praise, and thanks now and forever and ever.
- You can select prayers from section A and B of mixed categories; this is an all-time prayer.
- You can even select one prayer, think through it, and offer it to God.
- Sometimes we do not have a particular need of our own, and this can be a good opportunity to remember someone else's need. A good and effective prayer always starts with honouring and thanking God, so section A and B of mixed categories needs to be the first part of all prayers, and then you can add the requests from any other sections which are close to your heart.
- I invite you to use each prayer in the seven intercessory prayers separately. Alternatively, you can use each set or make your own intercessory prayers by using various prayers from any section. These can be used in your personal prayers or in your House Group or as a framework to lead the intercession during the worship at your church. The vast variety of prayers provided by the book can extend help in leading prayers for the school assemblies, the Christian Youth groups, the Sunday schools and the Christian unions.

The essential components of your creative prayer need to be based on the model of the Lord's Prayer:

1. Praise, worship, and thanksgiving to God the Father.

2. Our longing to see that God's will and His purposes are achieved through us for us, for the Church, and for the world.
3. To make confessions to God.
4. To depend on God for His promises, His provision, and His protection.
5. Responding to God's love and forgiveness and then to imitate God to do the same.
6. Deliverance from Satan, sin, and evil people.
7. Exalt and praise His name and leave the prayer before the throne of grace with thanksgiving in your heart. Amen.

Invitation to the prayer of commitment:

'I love the Lord because he hears and answers my prayers. Because He bends down and listens, I will pray as long as I have breath!' (Ps. 116: 1-2) Lord, I agree with the psalmist in making this prayer my own.

Note: All the verses from the Holy Scripture that have been quoted in this book are taken from New Living Translation, New International Version, Amplified Bible, Contemporary English Version, The Message, and New King James Version.

Chapter 1

Basics of Prayer

A. What is the true meaning of prayer?

Christian prayer is a spiritual activity of our expression to acknowledge who God is and what He has already done for us and to make our requests known to Him. This is how we can understand and define prayer. But the underlining truth is that prayer was first born in the heart of God and that in His love He created and saved us through our Lord Jesus Christ from our sins to have relationship with Him. So we are doing what we are created and saved for, and that is to pray or to communicate with God in His love and to have fellowship with the Holy Spirit through the grace of Lord Jesus Christ.

The main emphasis given by our Lord Jesus Christ on the power and the perseverance in prayer is in His authorisation to keep asking, keep seeking, keep knocking, and never to lose heart. The urgency for prayer can be stated by the fact that if there is no prayer, one could miss out on the divine pardon, protection, provision, and the divine nurture of our faith. This might seem to be an overstated fact, but opting out of prayer could either be a sign of ignorance or disobedience to the command to pray or a sign of total dependence on self and not on God.

The Almighty has the power to move mountains in our lives, and a prayer in faith can move the heart of the Almighty. God is not only committed to hear and answer the prayers of His people, but He is also able to accomplish far more than we can dare to ask or imagine.

B. What is the necessity and the importance of prayer?

The following passages from the Holy Scripture supports and affirms the necessity and the importance of prayer. The purpose of this book is not to provide you with full study or teaching on prayer but to encourage the readers to soak themselves in God's Word concerning prayer. The foundation of true prayer is laid down with serious hearing, reading and learning, studying and reflecting God's Word. The Holy Spirit teaches us how to pray by using the Word of God that He himself has inspired. It is through His own Word that God reveals His character which stimulates us to give God worship, adoration, and praise. It is God's Word that reveals to us the knowledge of His will and His promises, and that gives us the subject and the content of our prayers. It is His Word that gives us the strong desire and the longing to see that God's plans, purposes, and promises are fulfilled. We need to hold on to the truth that God's Word and prayer work together. Both God's Word and prayer fully complement, supplement, and support each other.

Sometimes it is beneficial to read a particular passage of the Bible to yourself aloud and slowly. Repeating it several times could help to let it sink in your head and in your heart. You are invited to try with the sixteen verses selected below.

Some passages from the Word of God have been selected to support and affirm the necessity and the importance of prayer. They are as follows:

1. *Whenever two or three of you* **come** *together in my name,* **I AM there with you.** (Matt. 18: 20)
2. Lord Jesus Christ said, '*I will do whatever you* **ask** *in my name,* **so that the Son may bring glory to the Father.**' (John 14: 13)
3. *Let us* **come boldly** *to the throne of our gracious God.* **There we will receive His mercy, and we fill find grace to help us when we need it**. (Heb. 4: 16)
4. *O my people have* **confidence** *in the Lord your God at all times;* **pour your hearts before Him**; **for He is your security and your refuge.** (Ps. 62: 8)
5. *Do not be anxious about anything, but in everything, by prayer and petition, with thanksgiving,* **present** *your requests to God.* **And the**

peace of God, which transcends all understanding, will guard your hearts and your minds in Christ Jesus. (Phil. 4: 6-7)
6. *The **earnest prayer** of a righteous person **has great power and wonderful results.*** (James 5: 16^b)
7. ***Ask and it will be given to you; seek and you will find, knock and it will be opened for you.*** (Matt. 7: 7)
8. Lord Jesus Christ commanded, '***Ask, using my name, and you will receive and you will have abundant joy***' (John 16: 24^b).
9. ***You do not have***, because ***you do not ask*** God. ***When you ask, you do not receive, because you ask with wrong motives, so that you may spend what you get on your pleasures.*** (James 4: 2-3)
10. This is what the Lord says; he who made the earth, the Lord who formed it and established it—the Lord is his name: '***Call to me and I will answer you and tell you great and unsearchable things you do not know***'. (Jer. 33: 2-3)
11. Lord Jesus Christ told His disciples, '***Pray that you will not fall into temptation***'. (Luke 22: 40)
12. *Without faith it is impossible to please God. For whoever comes to God must believe that God exists and **He rewards those who diligently seek him**.* (Heb. 11: 6)
13. *If my people who are called by my name will **humble** themselves and **pray** and **seek** my face and **turn** from their wicked ways. **I will hear from heaven and will forgive their sins and heal their land**.* (2 Chron. 7: 14)
14. *Pray at all times and on every occasion in the power of Holy Spirit.* ***Stay alert and be persistent in your prayers for all Christians everywhere.*** (Eph. 6: 18)
15. Concerning His Second Coming Jesus warned, '***Take heed, watch and pray; for you do not know when the time is.***' (Mark 13: 33)
16. *The Lord still waits for you to come to Him so that He can show His love and compassion. For the Lord is a faithful God.* ***Blessed are those who wait for Him to help them.*** (Isa. 30: 18)

C. What are the key points to effective prayer?

1. God in heaven hears and acts when people on earth call upon Him in faith and in expectation.
2. Come in the holy presence of God with reverence; bow not only the head, but also your heart in humility and in submission to His will.

3. Come before the righteous Father with your unworthiness and acknowledge that you are privileged to approach the holy God. Always remember with thanks and praise that this privilege has been obtained for you by the death, the resurrection, and the ascension of our Lord Jesus Christ.
4. Come to the all-knowing God and offer your prayers intelligently, precisely, concisely, and with sincere heart.
5. A good and a strong prayer is when there is more focus on the sovereignty of God and less on self.
6. God hears our unlimited prayers, when asked in accordance with His will.
7. The prayer with a clean heart and a clear conscience is the best condition for answered prayers.
8. Prayers are granted in the name of the Lord Jesus Christ. 'Ask in my name and the Father will grant you what you ask in my name,' Jesus Christ promised.
9. Lord Jesus Christ taught, 'I promise that when any two of you on earth agree about something you are praying for, my Father in heaven will do it for you.' So holding on to the promises of God and the agreement in the petition is vital for the results of our prayers.
10. Persistence in prayer is the key point; one has to keep on asking, knocking, and waiting on the Lord without losing heart. Blessed are those who wait on the Lord; they will find new strength. They will fly high on wings like eagles. They will run and not grow weary. They will walk and not faint. (Isa. 40: 31)
11. God still speaks to His people, and in prayer His people need to have pure, thirsty, sensitive, and listening heart.

D. What are the different types of prayers?

1. The number one priority as a Christian is to focus on who God is and offer Him *the worship and adoration* that is due to Him.
2. God has done so much for us in the past; He is already doing wonderful things at present and has promised to do far more for the future than we can comprehend. Therefore, *God is worthy of all our praise and thanks.*
3. We are commanded to bring our *requests and petitions to God*; this pleases the Father.

4. If we confess our sins, God is faithful and just to forgive us and cleanse us from all unrighteousness. Self-examination and the *prayer of confession* keep us away from sin and closer to God.
5. *Listening prayers* takes place when we read and study God's Word prayerfully.
6. *The intercessory prayers* are offered to God on behalf of other people's need instead of focusing on our own needs. The Lord is seeking to employ more labourers in the ministry of intercession. I am challenged, and I am aware of the need for myself and for the other Christians to learn more about the intercessory prayers.

E. What is intercession?

A perfect example of intercession is set by our Lord Jesus Christ. In Luke 22: 31-32, Jesus prayed for Peter that his faith should not be destroyed by Satan but that his faith be renewed.

Intercession is exemplified, and true love, concern, and care are demonstrated by our Lord Jesus Christ in John 17: 9-25. Jesus is praying to His Father for His present and for His future believers, which includes us too. The content of His prayer is that they would stay faithful to the revelation of God which Jesus gave them and that they will advance in holiness by abiding in the truth. Jesus is asking His Father for their protection from the power of the Evil One (who is still prowling like a lion to destroy and to devour us) and that they will abide in the Word of God so that they are kept away from sin. The last part of His prayer is for the unity in their faith and in their love for God and for each other. Finally, Jesus prays that all those who believe in Him will share His glory with Him.

Lord Jesus Christ interceded for us when He was on earth, and now He is back on His throne sitting on the right hand of God the Father. He is still interceding in the same manner as He did on earth. 'Because Jesus lives forever, he has a permanent priesthood. Therefore he is able also to save them to the uttermost that come unto God by him, seeing he ever lives to make intercession for them' (Heb. 7: 24-25).

Roman 8: 26-27 assures us that the Holy Spirit is also interceding for us in our hearts, so we need to take courage and to praise and thank our God for His faithfulness that we are continually empowered and protected by the living and eternal Saviour in heaven and by His Spirit on earth. We are called to imitate and to obey our Lord Jesus Christ; so my brothers and my sisters in Christ, let us accept the challenge, and in the power of the Holy Spirit, let us devote and commit ourselves for this ministry of intercession for others. Let us submit ourselves to God and to resist the devil by the power provided from above, and he will flee from us.

Christians are created, chosen, and employed by God to intercede in prayer. So the prayer with concern and care and love for others is not only essential, but also a privilege and a responsibility of true Christians. It is beyond our understanding of how the most powerful and most wise God works His purposes and plans through our prayers.

Here are some key points on intercession that might help those who are seriously thinking to make a commitment to be an intercessor or want to grow deeper in their intercessions:

1. In intercessions, we come to the ultimate source of authority, power, provision, and protection, knowing that God will intervene and bring the necessary change.
2. The foundations of intercessory prayers are based on who Jesus is and what He has accomplished. *The following are the true and powerful facts which give us the power, the confidence, and the authority to our prayers:*

    - Jesus has come not to destroy but to give life to the full.
    - Jesus has come to seek and to save that was lost and condemned.
    - Lord Jesus Christ has all authority in heaven and on earth.
    - 'When people keep on sinning, it shows they belong to the devil, who has been sinning since the beginning. *But the Son of God came to destroy the works of the devil.* Those who have been born into God's family do not make a practice of sinning, because God's life is in them' (1 John 3: 8-9).
    - Remind yourself and give thanks for this truth that by the death on the Cross and by the power of His resurrection Lord Jesus Christ has already won the victory over Satan, sin, and death.

- Greater is the living Christ in us than the Evil One who is in the world.
- Lord Jesus Christ is our ever-living Saviour, king, and our eternal intercessor.

3. Prayer in the power of the Holy Spirit is the weapon which pushes back the lies, deception, and oppression of the Satan. Prayer destroys the influence of darkness working in our world. (Eph. 6: 10-18 and 2 Cor. 10: 4)
4. We need great intensity, passion, love, and compassion in offering our prayers. It is important that we identify ourselves with God's people and to share their pain, guilt, shame, and sorrow.
5. The intercession gives us the longing to see that God's will is done, His promises are fulfilled, and His name is exalted and glorified in all the earth.
6. The ultimate goal of true intercession is to have the desire to exalt God and to see Him being revealed and known to the individuals, to the churches, to the nations, and to the world.

'I urge, then, first of all, that requests, prayers, intercession and thanksgiving be made for everyone—for kings and all those in authority, that we may live peaceful and quiet lives in all godliness and holiness. This is good, and pleases God our Saviour, who wants all people to be saved and to come to a knowledge of the truth. For there is one God and one mediator between God and men, the man Christ Jesus; who gave himself as a ransom for all people' (1 Tim. 2: 1-6).

Chapter 2

Short Prayers of Mixed Categories

A. Praise and adoration to God

1. God the Creator, I worship and honour Your name because You made the heaven and the earth by the breath of Your mouth. What comes from the divine mouth is simply intelligent, powerful, beautiful, and eternal. Amen.
2. God of power and wisdom, accept my adoration and worship, because You are the creator of time, matter, space, and all the living beings. You are the only one who can sustain and uphold every created thing by Your wisdom and Your almighty power. Amen.
3. God Most High, You have unnumbered divine angels. They are Your created spiritual beings who serve You day and night. Yet You have set Your heart on the lowly and weak human beings. We give You all the praise and worship. Amen.
4. Praise God, Oh people! Let the sound of His praise be heard, for He has preserved our lives and has kept us on the right path! Amen.
5. Almighty God, I give You all the honour and praise, for You are holy and almighty, the God who was, who is, and who is still to come. So I pray, come, Lord Jesus. Come in Your majesty and power. Amen.
6. God our Saviour, I adore and worship with awe and amazement that You chose to become a human being for our sake. You chose all the details of Your human life from the birth to death, resurrection, and ascension to heaven from where You came. Thank You for being my God and my Saviour. Amen.

7. Lord Jesus Christ, You are so unique in every way that no one was like You. No one is and no one will ever be like You. Jesus, You are special and supreme. So all those who believe in Him, come with me and let us behold Him, bow down before Him, and adore Him, Jesus Christ the Lord. Amen.
8. My Jesus, my Redeemer, there is no one like You. I dare not compare You with anyone else. You are the only Saviour who gave Himself up for all generations, all peoples, and all the nations of the world. One day, every knee will bow before You. Lord, I can worship You for all eternity. Amen.
9. Faithful and unchanging Lord Jesus Christ, I worship and adore You because You are the same yesterday, today, and forever, and I can put all my trust in You. Amen.
10. I bow before the God-Man in worship and adoration for bringing God to earth and for taking our humanity to the throne of the God Most High. Unique Jesus, You have a unique love for us that You became a man for eternity and yet You are God, who is, who was, and who is to come, the Almighty One! Amen.
11. Jesus the Exalted One, You are worthy of our praise, worship, and adoration because You are superior to all other gods, angels, prophets, priests, and all religious leaders. You alone are the object of my worship. Amen.
12. Lord of lords, with all my heart I praise and worship You for the privilege that You have obtained for us that we can call God our Father. Now we have been given the right to be Your adopted children. Amen.
13. Heavenly Father, I am privileged and joyful that I can come in the presence of a holy and powerful God through Lord Jesus Christ. Nothing is more appropriate to offer You than my worship of awe and adoration. Amen.
14. Lord of eternal purposes, in worship I surrender my whole being to let You work Your purposes and Your plans in my life. Amen.
15. Oh Lord, the restorer of my life, I praise and thank You that You are the only one who can enlighten my soul, strengthen my life, and renew my heart. Amen.
16. King of Glory, I will praise You, Oh Lord my God, with all my heart. I will glorify Your name for ever because great is Your love towards me that You have washed away all my sins. Amen.

17. Yours, Oh Lord, is the greatness, the power, the glory, the majesty, and the splendour, for everything in heaven and on earth is Yours. Yours, Oh Lord, is the kingdom. You are exalted as head over all. Wealth and honour come from You. You are the ruler of all things. In Your hands are strength and power to exalt and to give strength to all. Now, our God, we give You thanks and praise for Your glorious name. Amen. (1 Chron. 29: 11-13)

B. Thanksgiving to God

1. The sacrifice that pleases You most is the sacrifice of praise and thanksgiving. So here I am offering the thoughts of my heart and the fruit of my lips to You, my Saviour Lord Jesus Christ. Amen.
2. Lord Jesus Christ, with all my heart I bring the sacrifice of my praise and thanksgiving for all You have achieved for me on that Cross. I just want to say that You are worthy of all praise. Amen.
3. Lord of priorities, thank You for directing me to reorganise my life's priorities. Help me to have the right balance in life, neither ignoring nor getting overenthusiastic about the various issues of life. I need Your discernment for choosing the right one. Amen.
4. God of wonderful surprises, I thank You and praise You for Your big and small blessings on occasions when I was least expecting and was prepared to carry on with the little I had. Amen.
5. I bless the Lord all the time because He has forgiven my transgression and cancelled all my sins with His own precious and holy blood. I worship my Lord who condemns me no more, for now I have His righteousness. Amen.
6. Accept my praise and thanks to You, Oh everlasting Lord, because when I was in distress and called upon You, You heard my cry and rescued me. Amen.
7. I thank You, my God, who is my ever-present help. I called You for help, and You came to my rescue and lifted me out of the messy situation I was in. Amen.
8. Lord of understanding, You gave me the clarity about the eternal life in Lord Jesus Christ. I humbly bow to give You praise that I didn't deserve this purchased and personal possession of eternal life. Thank You, Lord, that this eternal life is my present and my permanent possession. In gratitude, I want to help others to have better understanding of eternal life in Lord Jesus Christ. Amen.

9. Thank You, Almighty God, for our daily blessing in life which we enjoy but take them for granted. We thank You and praise that You are good towards Your creation. Amen.
10. Thank You for the gift of family, friends, neighbours, and the church members with whom we share our lives. Amen.

C. Dependence on God and calling upon Him for help

1. Hear my cry, Oh God and listen to my prayers. Besides You I have no one else. You are my only hope. Amen.
2. God of perfect harmony, I pray to bring harmony between my head, heart, and mouth, that my prayer will freely flow from my heart and head and then to my mouth. Amen.
3. Lord, even though I don't see much change in my circumstances, I am glad and thankful that Your Spirit prompts me not to lose heart but always ought to pray. Amen.
4. Righteous Father, whatever You do is right and just. Your love compels You to show Your compassion and power for those who cry unto You for help. Amen.
5. Lord, I am very disturbed within myself, but I turn to You for some comfort. Amen.
6. To You, Oh Lord, I lift up my soul. In You I trust, Oh God. Please do not let me be disgraced or let my oppressors triumph over me. Amen.
7. God of wisdom and love, show me Your ways and teach me Your paths and please guide me in Your truth. You are my God and my Saviour, and my hope is in You all day long. Amen.
8. Hear my voice when I call to You, Oh Lord, and be merciful to me and answer me, as I have been going through many troubles for a long time. But I am waiting for You to put an end to each and every one of them. Amen.
9. Lord, I am greatly encouraged by Your Word that You are close to the broken-hearted and strengthen those who are crushed in spirit. Jesus, please be my source of power, courage, and wisdom. Amen.
10. Lord God, please do not hide Your face from me and do not turn me away in anger. You have been my helper before. Do not reject me or forsake me now. Amen.
11. Lord, I am still confident of this that I will see the goodness of You in my lifetime. Wait for the Lord, Oh my soul, and be strong and take heart. Amen.

12. Hear my cry for mercy, Oh God of compassion and love. Please deliver me from liars and from deceitful people. It pains me to live with them. Amen.
13. God Almighty, please turn to me and be gracious to me, for I am lonely and afflicted. The troubles of my heart have multiplied, so I beg You to free me from my anguish. Amen.
14. Lord, You are my shepherd. Please guard my life and rescue me. May Your faithfulness towards me protect me from the power of darkness. Amen.
15. Lord, it is wonderful to know that the eyes of the Lord are on those who fear Him and on those whose hope is in His unfailing love. Amen.
16. Divine Teacher, I beg You to teach me Your ways, and only then I will be able to live my life in Your truth. I want You to give me undivided heart, that I may fear Your name. Amen.

D. Confession to God for the great need to live a true Christian life

1. Lord, please forgive me for not looking after my resources that well. Please help me to take my accountability to You a bit more seriously. May I be able to use my time, money, talent, and energy more positively and profitably for You, for my family, and for the community. Amen.
2. Lord, I come to You and bring the state of my heart at this very moment, filled with anger and annoyance, simply because I am being totally ignored and neglected. God the Holy Spirit, please guard my heart that I might not sin against You and Your people. Amen.
3. Lord, I confess to You that I have hopelessly spent too long looking at the closed door. Help me to see the new doors You have already opened. Thank You, Lord. Amen.
4. Lord, I am aware that I need to give my time to people, even if I only listen to their heartaches. But my biggest problem is that the busy life I live drains all my energy. So I pray, Lord, please equip me with Your love, which has time and energy for the needy people around me. Amen.
5. Father God, please forgive me for not paying much attention to show my Christlike love and sympathy to others. Help me to

support the vulnerable people for their particular needs without interfering with their private life. May I give them respect and dignity, which You have already given to them in Lord Jesus Christ. Amen.

6. Father God, I thank You for all the warnings given to us in the Holy Scripture. Help us, we pray that we will always make every effort to learn from our mistakes and try not to make the same mistake over and over again in order to avoid the serious consequences. Amen.

7. Holy Lord, we thank You and praise You for making us realise that what we put into our minds determines what comes out in words and actions. In the power of the Holy Spirit grant that we fix our thoughts on what is true, right, and honourable. Help us to think through the things that are pure, lovely, admirable, excellent, and worthy of praise. Amen.

8. God the Holy Spirit, forgive me for grieving You by the way I have lived my life. Please set me free from all the foul, abusive, and idle words I have ever spoken. Please replace it with the gracious, meaningful, encouraging, and positive words so that whoever hears what comes from my mouth will be helped and blessed. Amen.

9. Lord Jesus Christ, sometimes I tremble at the warning You have given me, that one day I will have to give an account of every careless word I have ever spoken. Lord, I am guilty, and I need the cleansing of my heart and of my lips. I am in desperation. I invite You, God the Holy Spirit, to fill me with pure attitudes and motives, and cleanse my heart and my speech by the blood of Lord Jesus Christ. Amen.

10. Oh Lord, I call to You to set a guard over my mouth and to keep watch over the door of my lips. Let not my heart be drawn to what is evil or to take part in the evil deeds with people who are evildoers. May all I say with my mouth bring honour and glory to Your holy name. Amen.

11. Lord, I want to honour and bless You with my tongue by speaking out all the wonderful things You have done for me. Amen.

12. Living Saviour, I need Your help to fight the good fight of faith. Grant that I take it as a sacred task of guarding the truth You have entrusted me in Lord Jesus Christ. Amen.

13. Lord Jesus Christ, I pray to guard my heart and my mouth because it affects everything I say and do. Amen.

14. Lord Jesus Christ, I pray that You grant us the spirit of truth, honesty, purity, integrity, gentleness, compassion, obedience, and forgiveness. We confess that we are in great need of these qualities. Amen.
15. Lord, I am determined not to sit back and sulk but to keep on praying and waiting on You until You give me the freedom and the power which is much needed in my life. Amen.
16. Lord, I do confess with all my heart that one touch of the Lord Jesus Christ can change life for eternity. Today I have come to receive that unique touch from You. Amen.
17. Oh my soul, why are you so stubborn and proud. Arise. Just touch the hem of His garment in faith. Lord, open the eyes of my heart that I will understand and know You more. I lift up my hands just to tell You that, Lord, I love You with all my heart. Amen.
18. Lord, I confess that sometimes when I pray for others, I pray without praying, because I fail to feel their pain and their desperation. So help me to be able to identify myself with them. Amen.
19. Lord, I admit that I find it easy to give my money, but I lack to show loving, tender care towards them. Help me to overcome this issue. Amen.

E. Forgiveness of God to us and our forgiveness to others

1. Thank You, Lord Jesus Christ, for saving me from the power and the penalty of my sins. Equip me with Your power to live this new life for Your glory. Amen.
2. Father, my heart is full of awe and joy that You gave Your Son Jesus as a sacrifice for my sins and the sins of the whole world. Thank You, Lord Jesus Christ, for obtaining my forgiveness. I receive Your forgiveness. Amen.
3. Lord Jesus Christ, You have set up a high standard of forgiveness from the Cross when You were tortured, insulted, and dehumanised. Yet your prayer was 'Father, forgive them, for they do not know what they are doing.' Empower me, please, to follow Your example. Amen.
4. Merciful Father, I thank You that by Your holy blood, I am forgiven. I pray, please help me to search my heart today if there is any sin of unforgivingness on my part that I need to confess and to be cleansed from. Amen.

5. Righteous Father, You grant mercy to those who are merciful, so, I pray, set me free from any resentment, hatred, and bitterness for others and grant me a renewed and a forgiving heart. Amen.
6. Holy Spirit, help me to forgive others as I am forgiven by the Lord Jesus Christ, even if I have to forgive others seventy times seven. Amen.
7. Lord, I need Your grace not to look down on other people's foolish mistakes. I confess that in my weak humanity I could have done the same. But I do pray, please make us strong and wise to stand against all temptations, which could lead us to the wrong path. Amen.
8. Lord Jesus Christ, I thank You and praise You for forgiving all my sinful past. But I find it hard to forgive myself, so I pray for Your power to enable me to do so. Amen.
9. Father God, Your goodness is the same towards evil and good people, just and the unjust. Like a true child of God, help me to do my best in loving and praying for those who misuse my generosity. I sincerely pray that I need to show my goodwill towards my enemies. Amen.
10. Lord, by Your grace I can just manage to forgive others, but I do find it hard to forget their offences and the pain inflicted on me. Lord, in Your love, holiness, and justice, You forgive all ours sins, You cleanse us from all our wickedness, and then in Your memory You keep no record against us. Enable me that in Your power I could do the same. Amen.

F. Provision of God (for all our needs)

1. Let us approach the throne of grace with confidence, so that we may receive mercy and find grace to help us in time of need. (Heb. 4: 16)
2. Hear, Oh Lord, and answer me, for I am desperate and needy. Please guard my life, for I am devoted to You. Amen.
3. God the Provider, I pray for the provision of a new job as I cannot carry on any longer without a job. Please hurry. Amen.
4. Lord, please provide an opportunity for me to earn little more money for my growing family. Amen.
5. God the Father, please help me to trust Your Holy Scripture and believe what You have said concerning my needs. May I be able to

hold on to the promise that You will supply all my needs according the riches of Your glory. Amen.

6. It is also wonderful to know that when You did not spare Your Son Jesus Christ and gave Him for us all, with Him You will not hold back other things. So I will wait in expectation with thanksgiving in my heart. Amen.

7. Lord of life, I come before You in my old age and hold on to Your promises that as You have cared for me since I was born, You will be faithful towards me and uphold me until I finish the race of my life. Amen.

8. Lord, I stand on the crossroads of my life, looking for new direction in my career. Lord, help me to believe and to have confidence that You know the plans You have for me. So please lead me day by day into that direction. Amen.

9. Lord Jesus Christ, I pray to grant us the spirit of truth, honesty, purity, integrity, gentleness, compassion, obedience, and forgiveness. Lord, this we need, and we depend on You. Amen.

10. Lord, I bring my sleepless nights of worrying about the circumstances which are out of my control. I pray, tonight I will lie down in peace, trusting that all things that happen to me are in Your control. Lord, please make me dwell in safety that I will wake up all sustained and encouraged. Amen.

11. Lord my God, I pray to grant me the confidence and the trust in You that You will definitely supply all my needs from Your glorious riches along with the wonderful blessings that comes by knowing the Lord Jesus Christ. Amen.

12. God the Provider and the Sustainer, grant me strength, courage, and the ability to be able to carry on with my daily tasks. Amen.

13. God my Creator, help me to trust and depend on You more so that I will not worry for those needs You have promised to supply. Amen.

14. Lord, I want to be confident that You will supply all my needs from the riches of Your glory. Oh Lord, I do believe, but help my unbelief. Amen.

15. Lord, I believe that You have already prepared all we need, spiritually, mentally, emotionally, and financially, for this life. This brings great comfort for us, but I know that the best is yet to come. As it says in Your Word, 'No eye has seen, no ear has heard, and no mind has conceived what God has prepared for those who love Him.' Amen.

G. Protection of God (in sufferings/temptations/tests)

1. Lord of unshakeable kingdom, You are my hiding place, and I come to You for protection. You will surround me with the songs or slogans of deliverance. Amen.
2. Suffering Servant and yet the King over all, when I focus on the Cross that You died, I adore and thank You that Your plans are extraordinary and above all human wisdom. You work through the medium of pain, humiliation, and suffering, but the end result is eternally beautiful, joyful, powerful, and fruitful for the whole world. Amen.
3. Triumphant Lord and living Saviour who has the power and the authority in heaven and on earth, come and set us free from the spirit of lies, deception, and destruction. And give us freedom from the spirit of decrease, hatred, hardness of heart, and disobedience which works in our world and causes us all kinds of pain and suffering. Amen.
4. In my suffering caused by others, I call upon the righteous Father to supply me with endurance, courage, forgiveness, and understanding so that I will let You have Your way in my life—all for Your glory and for my blessings. Amen.
5. Lord, there is so much hurt in the married life of many Christian couples. Lord, help them to keep a watch over their spirits by staying under the influence of Your Holy Spirit. Lord Jesus Christ, You are the restorer of all relationships. Please do the same for them too. Amen.
6. Lord, the suffering You sent was good for me, for it taught me to pay attention to Your principles. It amazes me that You always bring good out of the bad things that happens to us. Amen.
7. Lord, before I was tested, I went astray, but my troubles turned out all for the best—they forced me to depend on You. Amen.
8. Lord of true love, I bring those who have been abused both mentally and physically in their love affairs and have lost total trust in all human beings. Please grant them courage, wisdom, and strength that by Your love and power they will be able to move on in their lives. Please bring the genuinely loving and faithful people in their lives. Amen.
9. Lord, I pray for those who are the victims of the selfish love with the wrong motives. Oh Judge of all people, look with mercy and

come to the defence of those who have been cheated in their love relationship. Amen.

10. Divine Master, we call upon You for those who are treated badly and paid unfairly in their workplaces. Lord, please put the fear of You in the hearts of those who are responsible for bringing pain to others. May there be mutual respect, cooperation, and healthy environment in all working places all over the world. Amen.

11. Oh Lord, I thank You and praise You for Your abounding grace that is sufficient for me and for my circumstances, because Your power effectively works in my weakness and in my needs. Since I know that it is all for Your glory, may I be able to delight in my weaknesses, insults, hardships, persecutions, and difficulties. Amen.

12. I am triumphant, Lord Jesus Christ, knowing that You have victoriously defeated Satan and destroyed the works of the devil. I come for Your protection to deliver us from the Evil One. Amen.

13. Lord, we pray that You will protect us from the wrong exposure to the things of this world. Grant us wisdom and courage to make the right choices wherever it is possible. Amen.

14. Grant us the spirit of awareness and discernment so that we will not be manipulated by the media and will not be captured by the deception, which can take us away from the Christian values. Amen.

15. 'No temptation has seized you except what is common to people. And God is faithful; he will not let you be tempted beyond what you can bear. But when you are tempted, he will also provide a way out so that you can stand up under it' (1 Cor. 10: 13). Lord, this is my prayer. Amen.

16. 'Let us run with endurance the race that God has set before us. We do this by keeping our eyes fixed on Jesus, on whom our faith depends from start to finish. He was willing to die a shameful death on the cross because of the joy he knew would be his afterwards. Now he is seated in the place of highest honour beside God's throne in heaven. Think about all he endured when sinful people did such terrible things to him, so that you don't become weary and give up' (Heb. 12: 2-3). Lord, thank You for this passage. Please strengthen me through it. Amen.

H. Church of God

1. Lord of the Church, we pray for the persecuted churches all over the world. May they experience Your presence and Your power during their trials and their sufferings. We seek Your protection and justice they require. Oh Lord, hear our petition for them. Amen.
2. Father of all compassion and God of all comfort, we bring the suffering churches before You. Please equip such believers with courage, strength, and perseverance. Amen.
3. Father God, I request for the boldness I need to speak out for the weak, the underprivileged, and the defenceless. Amen.
4. Please fill me with Your power and with the passion for Lord Jesus Christ so that I will be able to proclaim the good news of salvation through our Lord Jesus Christ. Amen.
5. Creative God, we thank You and adore You for all those who are sincerely using the modern technology for bringing the blessings of the Lord Jesus Christ to the people impossible to reach otherwise. Amen.
6. Lord, I pray that may the Church avail all the resources, opportunities, and advance means for spreading and sharing the good news of Lord Jesus Christ. Amen.
7. Lord, please grant all Christians with the spirit of discernment that we will not be manipulated by the secular media. With Your power, please keep us alert and strong that we are not captured by the deception, which can easily take us from the Christian values. Amen.
8. Lord, I pray that may the heart of the Church set on fire with the love for the Lord Jesus Christ and great enthusiasm for His zeal and for His passion. Amen.
9. Lord, as Apostle Paul prayed for the Church, I pray, please grant the Church a spirit of wisdom and revelation so that Christ will be known better by the Church. I pray that the Church will be flooded with the light of Christ in order to know and to appreciate the hope of glory we have in our Saviour Lord Jesus Christ. Amen.
10. I praise You, Creative God, for the good use of the Internet. Those who live in fear but in the comfort of their privacy can have access

to Your Word through the Internet. Bless Your Church for this provision. As a result, thank You, Father, that many are finding the truth in the person of Lord Jesus Christ. Hallelujah! Praise the Lord! Amen.
11. Lord, I pray for the community I live in. May our community experience the awareness of Your presence around them. May they feel the need for the living God in their lives. Please equip Your Church to meet the spiritual needs of their community. Amen.
12. Lord Jesus Christ, I pray that may You shake the Church so that all that is of the world will fall and all that is of You will remain and bear fruit for Your glory. Amen.

I. Confidence in God and in His promises

1. 'I tell you the truth that if two of you on earth agree about anything you ask for, it will be done for you by my Father in heaven. For where two or three come together in my name, there *am I* with them' (Matt. 18: 19-20). Lord Jesus Christ, I thank You and praise for this particular promise. Amen.
2. Jesus the Messiah, the Son of the Most High, You have declared that the Church belongs to You and You will build Your Church and all the powers of hell will not be able to conquer it. Thank You for this confidence we have in You that the foundation upon which the Church is building and growing is the unshakeable Rock. Jesus, the Lord of the Church, You are that Rock. Hallelujah! Amen.
3. God Almighty, I thank You and praise You that there is nothing difficult for You, because everything is possible for You. This truth activates my faith for my prayers, and I am grateful to You. Amen.
4. When the Lord is with me, who can stand against me? Nothing can separate me from the love of God. Amen.
5. In my weakness I forget Your faithfulness, so please help me, Lord Jesus Christ, to stay closer to You. Grant that I will hold on to Your promise that You will never leave me nor forsake me. Amen.
6. Faithful and true God, we honour Your name that in Lord Jesus Christ You have fulfilled Your promises to us. May we now hold on to the promise of His Second Coming by preparing ourselves to welcome Him back as our Judge and our King. Amen.

7. Lord, I want a constant reminder that I am loved by Your unchanging and powerful love and that I am a very precious possession of Yours bought by You by the Holy blood shed on the Cross by Jesus Christ. I am Yours for all eternity. Amen.
8. God the Holy Spirit, please help me to read and frequently repeat Your promises to myself so that Your truth in my life is established. Your words have authority and power, so enable me to focus and to hold on to Your Word in my head and in my heart. Amen.
9. Lord, thank You for the psalmist's confidence in You: 'I was young and now I am old, yet I have never seen the righteous forsaken or their children begging bread' (Ps. 37: 25). Lord, I am coming to You that You would please grant me the same confidence in You, as of the psalmist. Amen.
10. Lord, I need Your strength and courage to stay strong and steady, always enthusiastic about the Lord's work, for I know that nothing I do for the Lord is ever useless. Amen.
11. God my Creator, help me to trust and depend on You more so that I will not worry for those needs You have promised to supply. Amen.
12. The Lord has promised, 'I will forgive their wickedness and will remember their sins no more' (Heb. 8: 12). Thank You, Lord. Amen.
13. Oh Lord, I totally believe that You do answer the prayers of Your people. Amen.
14. Lord, I know in my spirit that the Lord is always with me. I will not be shaken, for the Lord is right beside me. Please empower me to hold on to this truth when the storms of life try to overwhelm me. Amen.
15. 'This is my command—be strong and courageous! Do not be afraid or discouraged. For the Lord your God is with you wherever you go' (Josh. 1: 9). Lord, please forgive me for disobeying Your command and for not making enough effort to come out of laziness, from my comfort zone, and from faint-heartedness. I desperately need Your help. Amen.
16. Thank You, Holy Spirit, for bringing me to this realisation that the great commission in Matthew 28: 18-20 applies to me as well. Lord, from now onwards I will go in the confidence that You have all power in heaven and on this earth, and I will hold on to Your

promise that You will always be with me in the presence and in the power of the promised Holy Spirit. Amen.
17. Lord Jesus Christ, help us to accept the reality of fear, doubt, sin, and struggles of life which are at war within us and against us. We confess that we have tried positive thinking, done our best to avoid conflicts, and have engaged ourselves in activities to make ourselves feel good. But Jesus, we have failed in our efforts and now turn to You because now we know that You are our refuge and strength, and You are our ever-present help. Amen.
18. Lord Jesus Christ, You are the Prince of Peace, and we come to You for power, inner strength, courage, security, love, provision, and protection which are some of the components of Your peace. Jesus, we thank You and praise You for the provision of this unique peace that only comes from You. Amen.
19. Lord of my peace, I have come to receive Your peace, which gives me the confidence that You are in control and that You are the Sovereign Lord. Your peace gives me the inner stability in knowing that God's kingdom is unshakeable and that my destiny in Lord Jesus Christ is determined and set. Amen.
20. Lord Jesus Christ, I praise and thank You for reconciling me with God. Lord, through You I have peace with God and His people. Amen.
21. Jesus, thank You for destroying the wall of hostility and establishing our friendship with God and others. Amen.
22. Lord, many times I have felt insecure and felt threatened of eternal harm by Satan. But today in my prayer, I come against this threat with the authoritative declaration of the Lord Jesus Christ. 'I give them eternal life, and they will never perish. No one will snatch them away from me, for my Father is more powerful than anyone else. So no one can take them from me. I and the Father are one.' I just bow my knees before You for this promise of safety and security that the Evil One cannot get his hands on me. Accept my gratitude for the assurance of my permanent life that I have by You and in You. Amen.
23. I am coming to you with this confidence that in Jesus, You are my Abba, my heavenly Father, and the Father of all believers. I am coming to receive the love, mercy, and grace because they flow out freely from Your throne. Amen.
24. The Lord is my light and my salvation—so why should I be afraid? Amen.

25. Turn us again to Yourself, Oh God. Make Your face shine down upon us. Only then we will be saved. Amen.
26. Lord God, I have confidence in You because You have all the power and the resources to answer my prayers. Amen.
27. I know that my God has all the capacity and the ability to hear and to answer millions of prayers at the same time. Amen.
28. Lord, sometimes I feel as if I am not making any significant progress in my spiritual life, and that distresses me. So I pray that You would give me the same confidence as Apostle Paul had in You and said: 'I am persuaded that God who began the good work within you will continue his work until it is finally finished on the day when Christ Jesus comes back.' Amen.
29. 'For the Lord gives wisdom! From his mouth come knowledge and understanding. He grants treasure of good sense to the godly. He is shield, protecting those who walk with integrity. He guards the path of justice and protects those who are faithful to him.' Lord, help us to hold on to our confidence in You by faith, by ongoing study of God's Word, and by praying, caring, and sharing. Amen.

J. Hindrance to prayers (unanswered prayers or delay in answer)

1. Lord, we confess that we complain when the answer to the prayer is delayed, when we know that our God answers the prayer of His people. Lord, give us a thankful heart for the loving and caring God who can be approached. Amen.
2. Lord, thank You for reminding us of Your Word, 'Before they call I will answer; whilst they are still speaking I will hear.' Father God, accept our praise because people have experienced that sometimes how swift Your answer was to their prayers. Amen.
3. Lord, thank You that sometimes whilst I was still praying, I knew in my heart that You had answered my prayers. Sovereign Lord, I will give You all the praise that only You know when or how to answer our prayers. Amen.
4. Lord, I acknowledge that in Your wisdom You have the reason and a purpose to delay the answer to my prayers. I beg You to show me if there is anything on my part which is a hindrance to my prayers. Amen.

5. Lord, You are neither weak to save me nor hard of hearing to listen to my prayers. The problem lies within me that my own sins cut me off from You. So today I turn to You and turn away from my sins and seek forgiveness in the name of the Lord Jesus Christ. Amen.

6. Lord, You already know the sinful state of my heart, and it is no good on my part to keep pretending that I am spiritually strong. I humbly confess that it is my sins that have hindered my prayers. I seek for the renewal of my heart. Amen.

7. I thank You, Lord, for speaking to me through Your Word: 'If I had not confessed the sin in my heart, my Lord would not have listened. But God did listen! He paid attention to my prayers. Praise God, who did not ignore my prayer and did not withdraw his unfailing love for me' (Ps. 66: 18-20). Lord, now I know that my prayers need to come from the pure heart and a clear conscience. I have sinned, and I need Your forgiveness and cleansing. Amen.

8. Lord, open my heart and my mind that I will understand the true meaning and the appreciation of Your forgiveness granted to me. Lord, I am finding it hard to forgive others. Please soften my heart to do so because the unforgivingness on my part is not the right condition for my prayer. Amen.

9. Help me, Lord, to make every effort to follow the teaching of Christ. So I must learn to prioritise the reconciliation by first forgiving and then praying. Amen.

10. Lord, I miss so much because I don't even bother to ask You. Please humble me not only to bring my needs in prayer, but also to ask for the right things. Amen.

11. Lord, I am ashamed to confess that most of my prayers had very selfish motive. But today my petition is to focus my prayers to seek Your kingdom to come in my own family, in my Church, in my community, and in my nation. Amen.

12. Lord, I thank You and praise You that I can depend on You for everything. But today my prayer is that You would give me the right desires and the right motives for my prayers. Help me to align my will with Yours in order to see the fulfilment of Your purposes. Amen.

13. As a child of the living God, I have the desire that may I get all the pleasure in obeying and pleasing You than seeking pleasure from the worldly things. So grant me a heart that is totally committed in the service of prayer. Amen.

14. Lord, please help the Christian married couples to examine their mutual respect and consideration for each other, because according to Your word in 1 Peter 3: 7, there could be a possibility of hindrance in our prayers. Amen.
15. Lord, You have made me realise that why some of my prayers are not answered because I prayed for my own glory. But now I bow before You and worship You and give You all the glory by confessing the wrong motives of my prayers. Amen.
16. Lord, I am praying and waiting for a long time, but there is no answer to my prayer. Lord, in Your power I am going to preserve in my prayer, and help me not to lose heart but to keep fighting against despair and hopelessness. Amen.
17. Lord, You have spoken to us through Apostle Paul (Eph. 6: 10-18) that we need to be qualified and to be prepared in the Lord Jesus Christ to stand firm and to resist against all strategies and tricks of the devil. Lord, I realise the importance, and in obedience I give myself in prayer to fight against all evil and wickedness. But in my own strength and power I can do nothing, and I desperately need the power of Your Holy Spirit. Amen.
18. Lord, thank You for revealing to me from Daniel 10: 12-14 that some of my prayers have been hindered by the challenge of the unseen evil forces. So please give me grace to resist these dark forces with fervent and earnest prayers in the power of the Holy Spirit. I know by faith that Your help is on the way. Amen.
19. Lord, You have been teaching me that prayer is a partnership with God. I have always prayed for my own agenda, which delayed Your purposes and the plans in the lives of the individuals, the governments, the nations, and the world. I offer myself in the service of prayer, in accordance with Your agenda. Amen.

K. Believing and using God's Word

1. Oh Father, grant that when I open the pages of the Holy Bible, I will have a strong conviction and realisation that I am reading Your message just for me. Amen.
2. God the Father, draw me closer to You through Your Word. Your Word is truth and life to me. I want to be a Bible-minded person so that I am wise, bold, and steady. Amen.

3. Lord God, I have no words to express my gratitude for the Holy Scripture in my own language. Accept my thanks for the availability of Your eternal and precious Word, which You have protected and preserved for all the generations, for all the nations, and for all the people. Amen.
4. God the Holy Spirit, I pray that You will open my understanding so that I can fully grasp the whole truth revealed in the Holy Bible. Amen.
5. Spirit of the living Saviour, I pray for the spirit of diligence that I will not only read, but I will also spend time and energy to dig into Your Word. Amen.
6. Lord, I sincerely read my Bible almost every day. I gain knowledge of Your truth, and sometimes I am greatly touched. But my prayer is that I need a sensitive and a receptive heart so that I don't miss out on anything when You speak to me through Your holy Word. Holy Spirit, I invite You to open my ears and train me to be able to discern Your voice. Amen.
7. Oh Lord, enable us to put it in practice what You have already shown us in Your Holy Scripture what is good and what You require from us. You want us to act justly and to love mercy and to walk humbly with our God. Amen.
8. Lord, please help me to learn and to fully understand the importance and the meaning of this frequently quoted Bible verse, 'Man does not live on bread alone but on every word that comes from the mouth of the Lord.' Discipline me to daily feed on Your Holy Word. Amen.
9. Lord, I do believe that Your revealed Word in the Holy Scripture is inspired and trustworthy. Help me to make it useful for myself and for others and to learn and to teach all that is true and right. Your Word is a powerful tool and a perfect guide for realising mistakes, for correction, and for training in the righteous things of God. Amen.
10. God Almighty, we thank and praise You for counting us worthy to receive Your inspired Word given to us in the Holy Bible. May we handle Your Word with great reverence and care so that we do not distort its message. Give us the courage to stand up and

confront those who bring insults to Your Word or misuse it for their benefits. Amen.

11. Sovereign Lord, give me an instructed tongue so that I am always ready to speak the word in season to them who are weak and weary due to the burdens of life. Amen.

12. Lord, You have challenged me with Your words that if I don't love the people I see and live with, how can I possibly love the invisible God who lives in me? Holy Spirit, please pour the love of God in my heart that I will be able to love God and His people. Amen.

13. Lord, I pray to You that in Your love and power, You will strengthen my feeble hands and steady the knees that give away. Please encourage my fearful heart and make me a strong and stable person so that I do not live a fearful life. Amen.

14. Help me, Oh Lord, that when I come in prayer to You, I need to believe with all my heart that God exists and that He rewards those who earnestly seek Him. Amen.

15. Lord Jesus Christ the source of my faith, I turn to You to activate my faith to believe and trust that there is nothing too difficult for my God. Amen.

16. Lord Jesus Christ, the living Word of God, we thank You for the provision of Your Holy Scripture, which we read and learn every day. But our prayer for today is to give us the grace to put into practice and live out the essence of all we know and learn from Your Word. Amen.

17. Lord Jesus Christ, the living Word of God, I pray that may the pattern of my every day's prayer always be accompanied and supported by Your written and revealed Word. Amen.

18. Lord Jesus Christ, please grant that I will experience in my prayer life that God's Word is active and living. I am thankful to You with all my heart that You still speak to people, even ordinary people like myself, through Your Word. Lord, speak, for Your servant is listening. Amen.

19. Lord Jesus Christ, You are the only one who has the power and the authority to open my heart and my understanding. Please open my spiritual eyes and ears and give me a receptive heart for Your Word. Amen.

20. Lord Jesus Christ, You are still warning to all believers through Your Word, 'Watch and pray that you may not enter into temptation.' But Jesus in ourselves we do not have the power and the resources to be able to stay alert. So we look to You for that power to avoid any spiritual danger that can overtakes us by surprise. May we pray constantly for the divine assistance we need. Amen
21. My sisters and my brothers in Lord Jesus Christ, may the grace of our Lord Jesus Christ and the love of God and the fellowship of the Holy Spirit be with us all now and forever. Amen.

Chapter 3

Prayers Concerning Love

This is real love—not that we loved God, but that he loved us and sent his Son as a sacrifice to take away our sins.

(1 John 4: 10)

A. God's love for us

1. Lord Jesus Christ, we thank You and praise You that You didn't only defined and taught about love, but also You demonstrated Your great love by giving Your life as a ransom for the sinners. I receive Your love. Amen.
2. Father God, I worship and adore You for the gift of the Lord Jesus Christ and all the privileges which are granted with Him. Not that I owned or deserved this indescribable gift of Jesus, but You *loved* me so much that You *gave* Your *Son Jesus* that I will not be perished but will have Your life. Amen.
3. Lord, I do realise that there is no goodness of my own which could attract a holy God. But in the generosity of Your free love, You have showered the abundance of Your spiritual blessings upon me in Lord Jesus Christ my Redeemer. Amen.
4. Thank You, Lord that the true love, joy, peace, goodness, faithfulness, and self-control are the results of living a life under the influence of the Holy Spirit. Thank You for the gift of the Holy Spirit through our Saviour Lord Jesus Christ. Amen.
5. Father God, I pray for those who doubt Your love. Please turn their attention to the child Jesus in the manger. Enable them to behold

Jesus the man who died on that Cross as a sacrifice for our sins. It is here that You lavished Your love to the world by simply giving Your Son Jesus and demonstrated Your love, leaving no room to doubt Your love for us. Amen.

6. Help me, Lord, that I will not forget the encouraging word You have spoken to me, as Your child. The Lord said, 'My child, don't ignore it when the Lord disciplines you, and don't be discouraged when He corrects you. For the Lord disciplines those He loves, and He punishes those He accepts as His children.' Amen.

7. Grant us, Righteous Father, that we will be able to hold on to this conviction in our hearts and that nothing in all creation will ever be able to separate us from the love of God that is revealed and assigned to us in Lord Jesus Christ. Amen.

8. You are forgiving and good, Oh Lord, abounding in love to those who call to You. Listen closely to my prayer, Oh Lord. Hear my urgent cry for mercy. Bring joy in my life, Oh Lord, for I depend on You. I offer this prayer in the name of Jesus. Amen.

9. God, the source of love, I humbly come to You and seek for the impartation of Your love into my heart because Your love forgives, protects, provides, and gives respect and security. Your love is everlasting and remains undiminished. It is pure, kind, patient, true, supportive, and loyal. I am in need of this love. Amen.

10. May the God of love, grace, and light be gracious to us and bless us and make His face shine upon us. Amen.

11. Thank You, Father, that in Your love You created me in Your own image so that You could show Your love towards me. You love because You care for Your people. Amen.

12. I will praise You, Oh Lord my God, with all my heart. I will glorify Your name forever because great is Your love towards me that You have washed away all my sins. Amen.

13. Lord, have mercy on me because when I struggle to love my neighbour, I find it just impossible to love my enemies. So I pray to God the Holy Spirit to pour out the divine love in me so that I will be able to love and bless my enemies with Your supernatural love. Thank You for this provision. Amen.

14. Lord Jesus Christ, You measure my love for You by my obedience to Your commandments. Forgive me that I have fallen short and have lived my life how I wanted to live. But today I ask You to give me the spirit of obedience in my heart. Amen.

15. Oh Lord, righteousness and justice are the foundation of Your throne. Your everlasting love and Your faithfulness go before You. Blessed are those who have learned to acclaim You, and blessed are those who walk in the light of Your presence, Oh Lord. This is my prayer. Amen.
16. Oh Lord, accept our thanks and praise that we are not consumed by Your wrath because of Your great love and Your compassion which never fails, and there is a fresh supply of Your great mercy for each day. Amen.
17. I fall on my knees before the Lord of unfailing love and compassion, for You do not willingly bring affliction and grief to Your creation but show Your abundant love and mercy to all. Amen.
18. Lord of love, scribe it on the tablet of my heart and mind that You are the only one who truly loves me. But in my weakness I forget that I am a precious possession of Yours bought by the precious blood of the Lord Jesus Christ. Amen.
19. I adore You, Lord Jesus Christ, that on several occasions Your love became tangible to me through friends and neighbours. Amen.
20. Lord, I pray that You raise good counsellors who will encourage and strengthen people with the divine love of God, especially those who are broken and crushed in their spirit. Amen.
21. Lord, I adore You with all my heart that despite all my shortcomings, Your love for me never changes. In Your power and mercy I beg You to enable me to love You with all my heart, mind, strength, possessions, and time. Amen.
22. Lord, today I come to You and confess that every trial and grief in my life shake my faith to the extent that I start doubting Your love. I plead for Your help to deal with my doubt. Amen.
23. Father God, please help me to accept Your discipline and to know that Your discipline is the proof of Your great love towards me. Amen.
24. Lord Jesus Christ, please enable me to imitate You to love what is good and to hate what is evil. Amen.
25. Lord Jesus Christ, please enable me to imitate You to love others with sincere love, including my enemies. Amen.
26. Jesus, please open the door of my mouth to be able to tell everyone how faithful You are. Your love, Oh God is my song and I will always sing it. With the help of the Holy Spirit, I will never stop sharing the story of Your love that how You brought the salvation through Lord Jesus Christ. Amen.

27. Lord Jesus Christ, You said, 'I have loved you even as the Father has loved me; now remain in my love. If you obey my commands, you will remain in my love, just as I obeyed my Father's commands and remain in his love.' Thank You, Jesus, for setting an example, and so I pray to grant me the passion and the power to stay strong in Your love through obedience. Amen.
28. Lamb of God, in Your eternal love for me, You laid Your human life to accomplish the forgiveness of my sins. Please enable me that I will never stop giving You thanks and praise. Amen.
29. Lord Jesus Christ, along with the forgiveness of sins, in Your strong love for me, You desired to share Your divine life with me. In gratitude, I now worship and adore You, Jesus. Only You are worthy, our Lord and God, to receive the glory, honour, blessing, thanks, and power through the life I live in and for You. Amen.
30. Jesus the friend of all sinners, I am privileged, blessed, and highly honoured that You considered me to be Your friend. Lord, no one has greater love than Your love that You gave Your life for a weak, lost, broken, and helpless friend like me. Thank You for the work of restoration and transformation that is taking place in my life. I believe that one day this work will be completed to perfection. Hallelujah! Praise the Lord, now and for evermore! Amen.
31. Lord, I am grateful for Your eternal desire for me is to hear You when You speak. So I offer my ears and the eyes of my heart, which from time to time get blocked and dim due to my own sins. Lord, cleanse them with Your redeeming blood and anoint them with Your spirit. I am grateful that *Your love for me is so strong* that You never want to give up on me. Amen.
32. Lord, we pray Apostle Paul's prayer for the Church 'that may Christ make His home in Your hearts through faith. And I pray that You being rooted and established in love may have power, together with all the saints, to grasp how wide and long and high and deep is the love of Christ. And to know this love that surpasses knowledge—that may be filled to the measure of all fullness of God.' Lord, this is our prayer too. Amen.
33. Thank You, Holy Spirit, to teach us that true love is a capacity and a choice that only God has. God by sharing His image with us has also given us the same capacity to love. All praise, glory, honour, and worship to our God, as real love comes only from God. Amen.

B. Our love for God

1. The first and the most important commandment is to love God, and the second is to love your neighbour. Lord, have mercy on me and forgive my sin of reversing the order. Amen.
2. I bow down before You, Lord Jesus Christ, that in Your love You chose me to be part of Your family and to be part of Your kingdom. I am coming with inadequate and unspeakable words to thank and to praise that You live permanently in my weak and lowly heart. Grant me now the ability to abide in Your love and to serve You in obedience for Your glory alone. Amen.
3. Lord, Your Word says that those who obey God's Word really do love Him. This is the way to know whether or not we live in Him. I pray, grant me an obedient heart. Amen.
4. Lord, one way to love You is by sharing and defending the good news of the Lord Jesus Christ. Please equip me with the passion and the boldness that I need to do so. Amen.
5. God of love, empower me with Your Holy Spirit so that I will be able to have a genuine and sincere love for the Lord and will be able to hate evil and to love all that is good. Amen.
6. Lord of the law, it is encouraging and profitable to know that those who love Your laws have great peace and nothing causes them to stumble. Please give me the desire and the ability to love You with all my heart, soul, energy, time, and possessions. Amen.
7. Lord God, I thank and praise You that You have shown me what is good and what You require from me. So I pray that may You grant me the desire and the power to do what is right and to love mercy and compassion and live my life humbly with You, my God. Amen.
8. The Lord promises, 'I will rescue those who love me, I will protect those who trust in my name. When they call on me, I will answer; I will be with them in trouble. I will deliver and honour them. I will satisfy them with long life and give them my salvation.' I thank You and praise You, my Lord, that in Psalm 91, You have defined all blessings You grant to those who have set their love upon God. Accept my prayer of gratitude. Amen.
9. Lord, my prayer is that I will be able to love You by giving You all the worship and praise that is due to You. Holy Spirit, You are the only one who can prepare my heart to offer the worship that is acceptable to God. Amen.

10. Holy Spirit, please keep the fires of love for Christ ever burning on the altar of my heart. Please keep me alert to see that my love, my passion, and my zeal for Jesus will remain intense and untarnished. If there is any hidden sin working in my life, I need to be cleansed from all unrighteousness. Amen.
11. I adore and love You, Lord Jesus Christ, for You have the spirit of truth, life, renewal, restoration, transformation, abundance, and obedience. So I open my mouth for Your praise. Amen.
12. Lord, I praise You that Daniel pleaded in prayer as the result of taking God seriously. 'Oh Lord, You are a great and awesome God! You always fulfil Your promises of unfailing love to those who love and keep Your commands. Lord, everything You do is right, but show Your love, mercy, and grace to us because many times we have refused to listen to Your voice through Your Holy Scripture.' Lord, I make Daniel's prayer (Chapter 9) my own. Amen.
13. Lord, I want a constant reminder that if I don't love the people I see and live with, how I can possibly love the invisible God who lives in me? Amen.
14. Father God, please help me to love by doing Your will which You have revealed in Your Word. Amen.
15. Lord, Moses wanted to see Your glory and You described Your name to him and You have also revealed Yourself throughout the Holy Scripture that 'The Lord is compassionate, gracious, patient, holy, just, abounding in love, wise, faithful, true, and forgiving.' Lord, You reveal Your glory through Your character. I pray that one day in my love for You, I will give You all the glory when the Holy Spirit will change my character to resemble Yours. Amen.

C. **Our love for each other**

1. Jesus, I hear You saying, 'A new command I give you: love each other, just as I have loved you. By this all people will know that you are my followers.' Lord Jesus Christ, You have spoken these words to me before, but today these words are penetrating deeply into my heart and have challenged me. With Your help I will try to make every effort to demonstrate the Christlike love to prove the world that we are the true followers of Jesus. I pray that may I glorify Your name by doing so. Amen.

2. Lord, the source of all love, let the fruit of love be seen in my life. Amen.
3. Holy Spirit, please pour the love of God into my heart so that I will be able to love my neighbour as I love myself. Amen.
4. My prayer to You, Oh Lord, is that as I expect love and care from others, may I will be prepared to do the same. Amen.
5. Lord, may my love be shown in the act of my patience, kindness, and compassion towards others, including those who strongly dislike me. Amen.
6. Lord, what I need to ask You today is that in my love I should have strong awareness for the needs of others. I truly want to come out of my self-centred life and from my comfort zone, so I offer myself and all I have. Amen.
7. Lord, by Your love and power, may there be no traces of any kind of envy, pride, boasting, selfishness, and unfaithfulness found in my character. I offer the love in my heart for the purification. Amen.
8. Give me the love in my heart for others, the selfless love that is God-centred and others-centred. Amen.
9. Lord, in my spirit You are showing me that sometimes I pray without praying. I confess that I fail to have that intensity in my love and so failed to share their desperation and their pain. Grant me the compassion and the love of Jesus. Otherwise it is just impossible to do so. Amen.
10. Lord, I am not happy with myself that I find it easy and quick to give money and fail to add tender love and support to my monetary giving. Amen.
11. Lord of the Church, according to Your command You want to see the brotherly and sisterly love to be prevalent in our Church community. Help us to examine our love for each other and to make every effort to be able to put it practice. Amen.
12. Lord, we thank and praise You that there are some churches in the various parts of the world where love of Christ prevails amongst them. Bless them for their good witness and for giving You the glory for being a good model for other churches. Amen.
13. I am ashamed to confess that my love sometimes could be envious, boastful, proud, rude, and selfish. I invite You, Oh Lord, to come and to bring the necessary changes in my heart. Amen.

14. Lord of love, please help me to grasp the truth in Your Scriptures that hatred stirs up trouble, but love overlooks the wrongs that others do. Amen.
15. Lord Jesus Christ, my own human love is weak and tainted. So I am turning to You to please saturate my life with Your divine love so that Your love will flow out for others through praying, caring, and sharing. Amen.
16. Love always protects, trusts, hopes, perseveres, and supports. I strongly desire these characteristics of love to be the component of my character. Amen.
17. True love never takes delight in other people's sins, even the bad deeds of an enemy. So help me, Lord Jesus Christ, to pray and to bless my enemies for their repentance and for their forgiveness. Amen.
18. I have been deceived and robbed in every way in the name of love, and now I have lost my trust in people. Lord Jesus Christ, I also feel so insecure and vulnerable at the moment. I do not know what to do, and I am turning to You for help. Amen.
19. Lord of true love, I bring those who have been abused both mentally and physically in their love affairs and have lost total trust in all human beings. Please grant them courage, wisdom, and strength that by Your love and power they will be able to move on in their life. Please bring the genuinely loving and faithful people in their lives. Amen.
20. Lord, this is a prayer for those who are the victims of the selfish love with the wrong motives. Oh Judge of all people, look with mercy and come to the defence of those who have been cheated in their love relationship. Amen.
21. 'Husbands, love your wives as Christ loved you.' Lord, this is the most difficult thing to achieve, but I believe in Your power it is possible. Amen.
22. 'Wives, submit yourselves to your husbands.' Lord, it is quite difficult to understand what You meant by submission. I need Your understanding and Your love to be able to give my husband the right place in the family. Amen.
23. 'Let love be without hypocrisy.' Lord, I confess that I have no confidence to say that my love for others is always without pretence. I need You to deal with my motives to love You and others. Please give a genuine and a sincere love in my heart that is acceptable to You. Amen.

The final prayer concerning love:

This is how greatly God loved and dearly prized the world: that He even gave up His only begotten (unique) Son. And this is why: so that no one needs to be perished but by believing in His Son can have God's own eternal life. (John 3: 16)

Lord, in Your love and power help us to respond to Your gift of love in the Person of Lord Jesus Christ. Amen.

Chapter 4

Intercessory Prayers

Habakkuk's intercession: 'I have heard all about you, Lord, and I am filled with awe by the amazing things you have done. In this time of our deep need, begin again to help us, as you did in years gone by. Show us your power to save us. And in your anger, remember your mercy' (Hab. 3: 2; cf. Ps. 44: 1-3, 85: 6).

A. Prayers for the lost (in variety of ways)

1. God the Saviour, we pray for our world still lost in the ugliness of sin. Holy Spirit, make us desperate for our salvation. May You work in our hearts to turn us away from sins and towards the Saviour Lord Jesus Christ and into the kingdom of God. Amen.
2. Lord of contentment, sometimes it seems that we are lost in our worldly success, wealth, and possessions and now distressing others around us. Lord, grant us thankful, humble, and sensitive spirit within us. Please bring us to the realisation that it is pleasing to God when people are loved more than money or wealth or status. Amen.
3. Lord of all hope, I pray for those lost in the disappointments of life. Holy Spirit, please bring the right opportunities in their lives, give them hope, courage, and confidence to be able to make up what has been lost. May they focus on God for the missed blessings. Amen.
4. Lord of love and care, I pray for those who have been neglected and are abandoned by their loved ones or by the society. In their real life, they feel and behave like lost people. Lord, I have confidence in You that You never leave nor forsake anyone at any time. You

are the only one who is faithful. So make a provision of the right and sincere people to give support, love, and care to them. Amen.
5. Lord of life, I pray for those who have emptiness, discontentment, and insecurity in their lives. They are possibly lost in self-centredness or greed or dishonesty or low esteem or any kind of obsession in their life. I cry for mercy, Lord Jesus Christ. You are the only one who can satisfy them with Your own life. May they come to You to receive it. Amen.
6. Lord of comfort, I bring those lost in their long-suffering, which is not only causing them great pain, distress, hopelessness, but also resulting in confusion and doubt about Your love for them. Jesus, please be real to them and meet them where they are. Give them comfort, hope, courage, and strength to face their difficulties with Your power. May they come out from their trials with a renewed mind and strength. Amen.
7. Lord of all theology, we pray for those who are lost in searching and coining the theological terms and jargons. May they be able to focus on the simple and the powerful good news of the Lord Jesus Christ and then to receive and to grow in the new life of the Lord Jesus Christ for which He came. Amen.
8. Lord of the Holy Scripture, we thank You and praise You for the good Bible teachers and offer the prayer of protection upon them that they will continue to bring Your truth to people in the power of the Holy Spirit. But we do cry unto You for those who are overconfident in their own intelligence and reasoning in interpreting Your Word. Please grant them the humility to ask the Holy Spirit to open their understanding, in order to avoid the spiritual confusion in the Church. Amen.
9. Lord, we are so much lost in the rut of life that we find difficult to make time to spend with You and for You. Lord Jesus Christ the deliverer, I beg You to set us free from spending too much time in all the unimportant chores of life. So please help us to make that important choice of taking time to sit in Your presence. Amen.

B. Prayers for the sick in body, mind, or spirit

1. Lord Jesus Christ, the source of life, healing, restoration, and regeneration, You are the creator of all those who are either sick in body, mind, or spirit. You know the causes and the remedies, so

in Your love and power please turn towards them and give them a fresh touch of Your presence. I believe that one touch of Jesus can change everything for the best. Amen.
2. Lord of healing and wholeness, I pray for those who are terminally sick. May they feel Your presence every moment of their life. Grant them the faith to be able to fix their eyes on You. Help them to prepare themselves for the kingdom of God. Above all, give Your peace and strength to go through this tough time. Amen.
3. Lord of Peace, we pray for those who are suffering from some sort of severe disturbances in their mind and in their spirit. Lord Jesus Christ, in the power of Your Spirit reach deep down where the problem is and bring Your healing touch. Only You can give them the inner stability and the inner strength they need. Grant them a sound mind, sound emotions, and a sound spirit. Answer this prayer for Your own glory. Amen.
4. Lord, in Your mercy and love reach out to those who are so ill that we are not able to communicate with them. God the Holy Spirit, we turn to You to speak directly to their spirit all they need to know about Jesus. May Your kingdom come and Your will be done in their present suffering. Hear our prayer for the sake of the Lord Jesus Christ. Amen.
5. Lord of all goodness, forgive us that in human weakness it is so easy to blame You, when there is long-term physical, mental, or spiritual sickness taking control over us. Father, show Your love and power to bring healing and wholeness. Give them a sound mind and a sound spirit. Please bring something good and beautiful from their pain that will give You the glory and great blessing to them and those who serve them. Amen.
6. Lord Jesus Christ the wonderful Counsellor, we pray for all the Christian counsellors who are counselling those suffering from depression. Lord, give them wisdom and understanding from above so that they will be able to know the root cause and find solutions and the remedy from Your holy Word and through prayer. May the Christian counsellors themselves be a good model in the discipline of prayer and in the study of the Holy Bible. Amen.
7. Lord Jesus Christ the great physician, we thank You for Your healing through medication. We pray for blessing upon all those who serve us in the hospitals, in the local surgeries, and elsewhere.

Grant wisdom and clarity of mind to those who make the decision for the mode of treatment for their patients. Amen.

8. Lord Jesus Christ, please open the door of healing for those who are sick and frail in body or in mind and deliver them from all infirmities. Grant us the faith to believe that You are the source of healing and wholeness.

9. Lord of true discipline, we acknowledge we spend so much money, energy, time, and devotion which goes towards maintaining our physical and mental health. We are engrossed to look after our physical body at the expense of neglecting our spiritual health. We confess in the presence of Your Holy Spirit that we urgently need a thorough spiritual health check. Holy Spirit, You are an expert surgeon and a perfect teacher. So we surrender and submit ourselves to Your discipline and pray, 'Search us, Oh God and know our hearts. Test us and know our thoughts. Point out everything in us that offend You and lead us along the path of everlasting life.' Amen.

C. Prayers for creation and environment

1. Lord of the universe, we come in amazement that how much the whole universe display Your marvellous craftsmanship and declares Your glory. Please open our hearts and lips in praise to God who created everything by His divine utterance. Your unseen almighty and the creative power and the wisdom in that utterance have given us the visible and the functional matter (substance) that we take for granted. Humble us to bow before such a creator. Amen.

2. You are worthy, Oh Lord our God, to receive glory, honour, and power. For You created everything, and it is for Your pleasure that they were created and they exist. Yet it gives You immense joy to share Your creation with us, for our use and for our enjoyment. Create in us a thankful heart for Your goodness and for Your generosity. Amen.

3. Lord, You have graciously honoured the human beings with great authority and responsibility to be in charge of planet earth. Please help us to take our stewardship seriously because we are accountable to You. We confess that in one way or another we all have neglected our God-given duty. Please have mercy on us and forgive us. Amen.

4. God of revelation, Your purpose for the creation is to reveal Yourself through all that we see, touch, use, and enjoy. We confess that sometimes we do the opposite and deny and reject Your existence. In the power of the Holy Spirit and in Your mercy, open our hearts to acknowledge You as the creator and give You all the praise for which we are created for. Amen.
5. God the Father, You created everything visible and invisible through Lord Jesus Christ and for Him, and He holds all creation together by His power and wisdom. Grant us faith to acknowledge that You are the creator, sustainer, and the owner of this universe. Show me how I can be Your co-worker. I submit myself for Your service. Amen.
6. Lord, it is You who created the atoms, the tiniest basic building blocks of every matter or substance that exist in our universe. Lord, what You have created is mind-boggling that these atoms cannot be seen with the naked eye. Yet they have tremendous ability to produce unmanageable and unthinkable power and energy. Please grant us the responsibility that this power and energy will always be used for good and no more for the work of destruction. Above all, may You get the glory for this creation of Yours. Amen.
7. Lord God, You are the originator of all natural laws, all scientific knowledge, and its usefulness. But we are thankful for all the past, present, and the future scientists You have given us, who have spent their time and energy to discover those laws. Accept our thanks for giving them all the creative ability to invent useful things by using that knowledge. Forgive us that we take everything for granted and help us to give You all the praise and glory and bless the inventors. Amen.
8. We thank You and praise You for all the good and breathtaking films and TV productions on nature. Grant us a heart that will acknowledge You and will give the glory of what we see, learn, and enjoy from these wonderful series on nature. But we confess that we acclaim glory to the nature and to the mother earth. We rob glory from You and give it to the creation rather than giving praise and glory to the one who is the creator, the originator, the ruler, and the owner of the universe. In Your mercy forgive this sin of ours. Amen.
9. Creator God, draw our attention to Yourself—sufficient energy, power, wisdom, design, beauty, skill, variety, originality, and Your

goodness that is manifested in the creation of Your universe. Help us to understand that we need faith and not the wrong reasoning. We need to praise and not to oppose and rebel against You. Hear our prayers for the sake of Your glory. Amen.

10. Lord, create in us a new praise-giving and worshipping heart that will capture the glimpse of the glorious and the majestic Creator and God who gives and preserves life and is worshipped by all angels in heaven and people on earth. Amen.

11. Holy Spirit, I beg You in the love and mercy of Lord Jesus Christ to truly make me realise that You are the creator who gives help and hope to all people. You defend the cause of the weak and oppressed. You set free those who are spiritually bound and enlighten those sitting in the spiritual darkness of this world. Enable me to totally devote myself to such a Saviour. Amen.

12. Lord, help us to respect and look after all the resources that You have given to us. Grant us the responsibility to look after our earth and its environment but not at the expense of neglecting the Creator. Hear our prayer for the sake of Your holy name. Amen.

13. Lord Jesus Christ, we live in the decaying and the sinful environment of our world. But thank You and praise be to You, Father, that in Christ You have made the provision that we have the choice to live in the environment of God's presence. Holy Spirit, have mercy on us and enable us to respond to God's provision and to start living and enjoying the eternal life through and in Lord Jesus Christ. Amen.

14. Lord, You have promised to create a new earth and a new heaven. Your Word reveals to us that the sinful environment has brought decay and mortality to us and to all creation. Lord Jesus Christ, by Your eternal creative and the resurrected power, once again You will create a perfect earth and a new heaven and establish Your eternal kingdom in a perfect environment. But we need Your mercy for the sake of the Lord Jesus Christ that we will be ready to be part of that new creation. Amen.

D. Prayers for the nations and their governments

1. God of all nations, we pray that may all nations give You all the honour and glory, by acknowledging You as their ruler. Help them to live a godly life. Amen.

2. Lord, we pray for the peace of Jerusalem. This holy city belongs to You. May Your kingdom come and Your will be done in Jerusalem. Amen.
3. Jesus the King of the universe, You have given authority to all the governments of the world. We pray to grant the spirit of honesty and integrity to all those in authority. Deliver them from evil and make them strong in character so that they will not fall into the temptation of corruption. Amen.
4. We pray for all the governments that they will focus on the welfare of their people when every decision is taken and every law is made. Amen.
5. Lord Jesus Christ the Saviour of our world, we pray desperately for Europe for its financial security, for the genuine and strong leadership, and for the spiritual problems. We pray that all the countries of Europe will come before You in repentance and in confession of their sins against You and for the healing of their land. Amen.
6. We pray for all the Christian nations. May they continue to respect the Christian foundation upon which their nations were built. May they seek to pursue the true God in every aspect of their nation's life. May God always be honoured and exalted in their governments, in their culture, in their education system, in their police system, in their medical care system, in their judicial system, and in their churches. We fall on our knees and cry to You for the revival in all the Christian nations. Amen.
7. Lord Jesus Christ, the Prince of Peace, we pray for the unrest that is in the Middle East and in other parts of the world. May Your kingdom come and may Your will be done amongst these nations. May they come to know that You are the ultimate owner and the ruler of all nations and that You alone hold the future of each nation of the world. Lord, may the characteristics of love, mercy, compassion, justice, integrity, welfare, and peace be seen in these nations by Your power. Amen.
8. Lord of the poor, we plead to You in prayer for all the poor nations of the world. Grant wisdom, honesty, good management, and great sense of responsibility in handling the resources You already have given to them. May the appropriate help and support come from the rich and powerful nations. Amen.

E. Prayers for the Church

1. Lord of the Church, we thank You that You have rescued us from the present evil age. We pray that by Your power, wisdom, and discernment we will not again become the slaves of the world ruled by Satan. Keep Your Church safe from the Evil One. We ask this in the name of our Saviour and Lord Jesus Christ. Amen.
2. Lord, we are ashamed that we have been so preoccupied with our own activities in the Church and that we never paid any attention to the introduction of certain laws that have brought some decay, confusion, and chaos in the society. Father God, Your heart is saddened, but You are waiting to come back to our society, to our nations, and to our world to revive and regenerate our moral and our spiritual life. Yes, Lord, please come in the power of Your Holy Spirit to bring that revival which is mostly needed at this hour. Amen.
3. Church of Christ, I pray for you constantly, asking God, the glorious Father of our Lord Jesus Christ, to give you spiritual wisdom and understanding, so that you might grow in your knowledge of God. I pray that your hearts be flooded with light so that you can understand the wonderful future He has promised to those He called. I want the Church to realise the glorious inheritance He has given to His people. Father, we present Apostle Paul's prayer as our own prayer for the present universal Church. Amen.
4. We, the Church of the Lord Jesus Christ, fall on our knees and pray to our righteous Father that from His glorious resources He will graciously make us spiritually and inwardly strong by the power of the Holy Spirit. For Your name's sake we pray. Amen.
5. Lord of the Church, we pray that may each member of Your Church take their responsibility solemnly to preach the Word of God persistently wherever and whenever there is a God-given opportunity. Holy Spirit, we need Your help to prepare us for this mission so that we are always ready, whether the time is favourable or not. Amen.
6. Holy Spirit, sometimes we experience the spirit of confusion working in the Church. Give us clear understanding what the good news of Jesus is. Please make us strong that we will not compromise with the world's view of the good news. For the sake of Jesus, who is the good news for all the sinners. Amen.

7. Lord, we are ashamed that we deny Your uniqueness to please other people and include You as one of the many ways to God. Lord, in Your mercy forgive our sin of dishonouring and insulting the one who is the only Way to God. For the sake of Your glory, accept our payers. Amen.
8. Lord, forgive us that we are so devoted in running our churches that we are neglecting our responsibility of spreading and sharing the truth in the Lord Jesus Christ. Holy Spirit, we need strong passion and new commitment and a fresh touch of Your power. Amen.
9. Lord Jesus Christ, the living Word of God, we fall on our knees and pray that may the Church come back to the Holy Scripture. May we depend entirely on Your Word, in Your power, and in Your presence amongst us. Please protect us from the wrong reasoning and certainly from the strong world view of the morality and the salvation. Amen.
10. Lord of our prayers and the Lord of our faith, I have realised in my spirit that no one can pray unless they believe, and how can they possibly believe unless someone like myself tells them? How can I tell them when I am not equipped, prepared, and encouraged by my local church? Lord, in our spiritual weakness we have failed to grasp the truth that faith comes by hearing the Word of God. This faith is the key—to please God in processing our prayers. We are in great need for Your help, guidance, and passion. Lord, please come and mightily work through Your Church again. Amen.

F. Prayers for not taking God seriously or rejecting Him

1. Lord, we pray for those who reject the existence of God and when they feel thankful, they have no one to thank. In the difficult times, they are overwhelmed but no one to turn for help. Please break the hardness of their heart and grant openness in their spirit to acknowledge and to receive You as their God. Amen.
2. Lord, we pray for those who twist and try to corrupt the fundamental truth of the Christian faith through art and music, through the media of TV and films, and through the printed material. We pray against the spirit working in them and using them, but we pray earnestly for their deliverance from this evil. Have mercy on them and open the eyes of their heart to be able see that how they

are being used, in insulting and rejecting their Creator and their Saviour. Grant them a new heart. Amen.

3. Lord of reconciliation and restoration, we cry unto You for those who have been tempted, captivated, and trapped with the New Age religion. So they have left the true God out of their own lives. Holy Spirit, only You can redirect their path back to the Lord Jesus Christ, who is the only Way, the only Truth, and the only Life. Amen.

4. Lord of abundant life, we pray for all those who are spiritually dead that they don't even feel the need of God in their life. Holy Spirit, awaken them from their spiritual sleep. In Your power make them sensitive to the presence of God around them. In Your mercy grant them the awareness of their deep need to know and to enjoy the divine life available to them in Lord Jesus Christ. Amen.

5. We pray for those who hinder the work of evangelism and for those who persecute the Church. Grant them a sensitive spirit to realise that they are actually rebelling and opposing God and that one day, before His throne, they will be judged and condemned. Deliver them from evil and grant them a new life. Amen.

G. Intercessory prayers previously used in Sunday worship

Intercessory Prayer No: 1

Our Sovereign God, we come to You in confidence by making the prayer of King David our prayer.

God Almighty, You alone have the power and the greatness and the glory, the majesty, and all the splendour, for everything in heaven and on earth is Yours. Life and health, wealth and honour, strength and courage all are determined by You alone.

So we draw to Your throne of power and mercy with thanks and with great expectation, because You are the eternal source to meet all our needs.

Lord, in Your mercy, hear our prayer.

- Prayer for the world suffering from the conflicts and the wars:

Sovereign Lord of unlimited power, You are the refuge, strength, and an ever-present help in trouble. We bring all the people and all the regions of our world engaged in conflicts and continuous wars against each other. Lord, we believe that You have the power and the authority to totally end all the wars and to destroy all the war weapons. We pray for the speedy approach of such glorious days when You will give security and peace to our suffering world.

Lord, in Your mercy, hear our prayer.

- Prayer for the people suffering through the natural disasters:

The Sovereign Lord, the compassionate and gracious, who is slow to anger, abounding in love and faithfulness, forgiving wickedness and sin, we cry for Your unlimited mercy for the people suffering by the natural disasters. In Your sufficiency, please provide, protect, and rebuild the lives of those who are going through so much pain, distress, and hopelessness. Lord, grant that there will be unity, peace, order, and integrity amongst their people. In these difficult times may the people have a fresh touch of Your presence and power. May they be able to trust and depend on You more.

Lord, in Your mercy, hear our prayer.

- Prayer for the Church of Lord Jesus Christ:

Sovereign Lord of eternal plans and purposes, we bring the Church You have chosen for Your glory.

We pray that the glorious Father of our Lord Jesus Christ give His Church the Spirit of wisdom and revelation of His eternal plans and of His purposes so that the Church will come to know and please their Lord according to His own will. We pray that may the heart of the Church turn away from the worthless things. Grant Your Church, Almighty God, the protection from the compromise.

God the Holy Spirit, assist Your Church for the wholehearted commitment to the Lord Jesus Christ and to be faithful to their Saviour right to the end. Grant Your Church discernment so that the Church will seek to know and put into practice all that is true, right, pure, lovely, noble, and admirable, and then bring glory to Your name.

Lord, in Your mercy, hear our prayer.

- Let us pray for our parish priest.

God of appointments, we thank You and praise You for choosing our priest to serve You and Your people. Accept our thanks and praise for all the teachings, prayers, love, and support we all have received from him or her.

We earnestly pray for the commitment in his or her ministry. Please grant him or her all the wisdom, strength, courage, and passion that he or she needs. We submit him or her in Your care, provision, protection, and peace.

Sovereign God, we submit these prayers to You in the glorious name of our Saviour Lord Jesus Christ. Amen.

Intercessory Prayer No: 2

Concerning prayer our Lord Jesus Christ said, 'Pray in this manner . . . . 'We call it the Lord's Prayer. (This prayer has petitions concerning God and us.) We will pray through the seven requests in the Lord's Prayer, and those petitions are as follows:

God's fatherhood, God's preference, God's plan, God's purpose, God's provision, God's pardon, and God's protection

Let us pray . . .

God the Father, we bow before You with thanks and praise. We give You all the honour for Your love, which was demonstrated in the Person of Lord Jesus Christ. Through Him You establish the paternal relationship by adopting the believers as Your children. In the power of Your Holy Spirit help us to be committed, trustworthy, faithful, and obedient children of the living God.

Lord, in Your mercy, hear our prayer.

Lord Jesus Christ, we thank You and praise You for revealing to us and teaching us that God's priority and preference is to recognise and to honour God's majestic holy name. Please help us to capture this truth in our hearts and minds that we serve a holy God. Lord, please help us to give ourselves to You—to the one who is able to make us holy too.

Lord, we are aware of the fact that we have no changing power of our own. So give us the courage to submit ourselves to the Holy Spirit for the work of restoration and transformation. Grant us the urgency of keeping God's priority as our own by setting ourselves apart for God in order to proclaim, to serve, and to defend His holy name.

Pause . . .

Lord, in Your mercy, hear our prayer.

Lord God, may the whole world come to know that You are the King of our universe. We thank You and adore You for bringing Your kingship in our hearts, in our homes, and in Your holy Church through our Lord Jesus Christ. Grant us the understanding for the kingdom's agenda. Give us the direction and courage to help others to enter the kingdom of Your Son. May we devote ourselves in the preparation for the fullness of Your kingdom to come, when all sin and evil, all sickness and death, and all famine and starvation will banish. Thank You, Father, that in the kingdom of Your Son, life, wholeness, goodness, fullness, harmony, and peace will be restored for eternity.

Lord, in Your mercy, hear our prayer.

Lord God, may Your will be done in us, in the universal Church of Christ, and in all nations as it is done in heaven. Father, thank You and praise be to You that it is not Your will that any should perish, but all to repent and to have eternal life in Christ.

We pray for all the clergy and the ministry teams in our churches that they teach, preach, and counsel their congregation with great love, responsibility, wisdom, and courage. Please anoint each one of them with clear vision from above. May our worship give all the glory to God and bring fresh glimpse of Himself to us.

Lord, in Your mercy, hear our prayer.

God the Provider, the Almighty God, we thank and praise You with all our hearts for the provision of our Saviour Lord Jesus Christ. Through Him You have chosen us to be Your co-workers to help and to provide those in need. We bring those who are sick in body, mind, and soul, and in Your mercy provide the relevant healing and wholeness to each one of them.

Lord, in Your mercy, hear our prayer.

Lord, there is nothing we can perform to achieve the forgiveness for our sins. Father God, we thank You that when we confess our sins in faith, the blood of the Lord Jesus Christ cleanses us from all our sins. In receiving pardon from You, soften our hearts that in gratitude we can do the same for others. Lord God, please bring to our remembrance the person we need to forgive today.

Lord, in Your mercy, hear our prayer.

Victorious Lord Jesus Christ, we ask the prayer of protection and deliverance from the power of sin and death and from the power and deception of Satan. May we stay closer to You in prayer, reading, remembering, and studying the Holy Scripture. In these anxious times all over the world, may all people draw to You in faith for protection and security.

Lord, in Your mercy, hear our prayer.

Lord, the kingdom, the power, and the glory have always been Yours and will be Yours forever and ever. *Amen.*

Intercessory Prayer No: 3

In joyful expectation of His coming we pray to Lord Jesus Christ:

Maranatha!

Amen! Come, Lord Jesus!

Come to Your Church as Lord and Judge:

We pray to You, Lord Jesus Christ, to remind Your Church once again that You have all authority and power in heaven and on this earth. Please give us the assurance of Your sovereign rule or control over all people, all things, and all events. Help us to know that not even one atom in this universe is outside Your powerful dominion. Grant Your Church to experience His Lordship in this present age. May we long to welcome You as the Lord of the Church now and at Your Second Coming. Holy Spirit, grant us a strong desire to commit ourselves afresh to Your Lordship. As a judge, help us to live in the light of Your coming and give us longing and passion for Your kingdom.

Maranatha!

Amen! Come, Lord Jesus!

Come to Your world as the King of the nations:

We pray to You as the King of all kings. We lift You high for Your majestic greatness and Your awesome power over all nations. May Your eternal kingdom come and Your will be done in all the governments of the world so that people are governed with love, mercy, and justice. God the Holy Spirit, in Your mercy, please put the fear of the living God in the hearts of all in authority so that before You, all rules will stand in awe and silence.

Maranatha!

Amen! Come, Lord Jesus!

Come to Your people with a message of victory and peace:

We pray for those whose lives are devastated beyond their control, their loved ones killed and their homes destroyed by conflict, persecution, poverty, disease, and corruption. Lord Jesus Christ, we wait in anticipation of the coming of Your kingdom, where desolation is replaced by abundance and hope is brought to fulfilment. May we live in the realisation of Your victory over sin, death, temptations, and the Evil One.

Maranatha

Amen! Come, Lord Jesus!

Come to us as Saviour and Comforter:

Lord Jesus Christ, help us to remember that no matter how dark our situation may become, You will lift us above the storm and into the comfort of Your presence. Only You can take the burden of our sickness, pain, and tears. We thank You for the gift and the availability of Your Holy Spirit to be our comforter and helper at all times. So we pray that the God of all hope may let His love, joy, and peace overflow everyone present here.

Maranatha!

Amen! Come, Lord Jesus!

Come to us from heaven, Lord Jesus Christ, with Your majestic power and glory. Lift us up to meet You with the apostles Peter and Paul, with all the saints in Christ, and with the divine angels to live with You forever.

Maranatha!

Amen! Come, Lord Jesus!

Intercessory Prayer No: 4

As the Church is reflecting on the theme of healthy growth of the Church, so it is appropriate and relevant for us to focus all our intercessory prayers on this subject.

One of the biblical promises of an answered prayer is the agreement with the prayer, so when You agree with my prayers, the *response* will be, *Yes, Lord, this is our prayer*. When I say, *Lord, this is our prayer*, let us pray with intensity and with great conviction, for we know that we pray to the Lord who longs to hear and answer our prayers.

Let us pray . . .

Lord, You made it clear that the Church is Yours and that You are going to build her. Grant us a clear vision for the healthy growth of our Church, and may we totally do it Your way. Lord of the Church, please help us to realise that our health depends on what we focus on. We earnestly pray that, Jesus, may You be our focus.

Lord, this is our prayer.

Yes, Lord, this is our prayer.

Father, give us the heart to love Jesus as our Saviour and to worship Him as our Deity. Humble us to exalt Him as our Lord and to trust Jesus as our friend. Grant us the spirit to serve Him as our King and to be obedient to Him as our Master. Holy Spirit, please open our ears to listen to Jesus as our Teacher and our Counsellor. May we truly accept Jesus as our only Redeemer and be generous to share Him with others as the good news. May we not struggle but feel totally confident to depend on Jesus as the Eternal One. May our clear focus on Christ be seen and witnessed in our inspired worship, in all our church activities, and in our own lifestyle.

Lord, this is our prayer.

Yes, Lord, this is our prayer.

Father God, we thank You and praise You for taking our sins and our salvation seriously. Help us, Holy Spirit, to remember that we have an enemy, the old sinful nature, within us. Give us a strong desire to deal with our own sins every day at the foot of the Cross of Jesus so that our spiritual growth in the Lord is not hindered and retarded but will work towards holiness for which we are called. By the power of the Holy Spirit, please renew and transform us from within.

Lord, this is our prayer.

Yes, Lord, this is our prayer.

We worship You, Lord Jesus Christ that You came to destroy Satan, sin, and death, and You victoriously accomplished that. We come to You this day to receive Your power to live a victorious life so that we don't fall into the deception and the lies of Satan, who is the enemy of Lord Jesus and His Church. Holy Spirit, please equip Your Church so that we are always ready and prepared to resist the devil and never to compromise with him at any cost.

Lord, this is our prayer.

Yes, Lord, this is our prayer.

Lord, we thank You and praise for Your revealed and written Word in the Holy Bible. May we honour, trust, protect, learn, understand, and apply this precious gift given to us to maintain our health and growth. May we all be well rooted and well nourished with the Word of God.

Lord, this is our prayer.

Yes, Lord, this is our prayer.

Lord Jesus Christ, the source of all healing, we call on You for those on the prayer list. May Your healing touch bring healing and wholeness to their body, mind, and soul. May it bring glory to You and a great blessing for them.

Lord, this is our prayer.

Yes, Lord, this is our prayer.

Father God, finally we pray that may there be more group attendance for prayer and Bible study. Grant us love and generosity in our spirit to show more support and fellowship to those who are weak in faith. I pray that may evangelism be our passion and our natural lifestyle.

Lord, this is our prayer.
Yes, Lord, this is our prayer.
Amen.

Intercessory Prayer No: 5

- Let us pray for the Church of Lord Jesus Christ:

Father God, help us to keep our eyes fixed on Jesus, on whom our faith depends from start to maturity and to perfection. Father God, it is Your will that whoever sees Your Son Jesus and believes in Him has eternal life and You will raise them at the last day. Holy Spirit, please open our eyes. We want to see Jesus to reach out and touch Him and say that we love Him.

Lord, in Your mercy . . . hear our prayer.

- Let us continue to pray for the Church:

Holy Spirit, please open our spiritual eyes so that we can behold the face of the Lord Jesus Christ with our heart. Please transform and direct our lives as we learn to fix our gaze on the Lord who has the power to make everything new. Lord Jesus Christ, lift the veil of spiritual ignorance and bring to us the knowledge of Your truth in our heart. Lord, in Your power please dispel the fog of confusion that is produced by our own sins so that we can see God's work of salvation in Lord Jesus Christ and to respond to Him by receiving Him as gift that the *Father* offers to us.

Lord, in Your mercy . . . hear our prayer.

- Let us continue to pray for the Church:

Lord, help us to know and to understand the importance of looking into the face of Jesus which will help us to clarify that the Lord Jesus Christ is sovereign and that He is able and trustworthy to handle all the issues of our lives. Father, please grant that in Lord Jesus Christ may the Church find joy, hope, reassurance, and confidence in this day and age. We pray blessing upon this family who have honoured God by bringing their child to be part of Christ's Church. May they all grow in the knowledge of the Lord Jesus Christ.

Lord, in Your mercy . . . hear our prayer.

- Let us remember the people of Norway . . . .

Lord of comfort and peace, please comfort and uphold those who are hurting by the loss of their loved ones. Please also grant them Your peace and strength. Lord, we pray that may You bring some good out of this tragedy which took place last week in Norway. May Your kingdom come and Your will be done in the nation of Norway for Your glory and for their blessing.

Lord, in Your mercy . . . hear our prayer.

Lord, we pray for this individual who is responsible for the explosion and the shooting that took place a week ago in Norway. We pray that You bless him with the attitude of repentance and to open his understanding to know the truth in the Lord Jesus Christ. We believe that this truth will set him free from deception and destruction.

Lord, in Your mercy . . . hear our prayer.

- Let us pray for all those on the prayer list . . . .

Lord Jesus Christ, please open the door of healing for those who are sick and frail in body or mind and deliver them from all infirmities. Grant us the faith to believe that You are the source of healing and wholeness.

Merciful Father, accept these prayers for the sake of Your Son and our Saviour Jesus Christ.

The final intercessory prayer of blessing:

'May the Lord bless you and protect you. May the Lord smile on you and be gracious to you. May the Lord show you his favour and give you His own peace' (Num. 6: 24-26).

Intercessory Prayer No: 6

Let us pray . . . . (There will be long pauses to take time to participate in the prayers.)

God of all comfort, we pray for those amongst us going through distress, pain, anxiety, or illness. Thank You for being our God that we can depend on You. Please come today with love and power for healing, courage, strength, and relief.

Lord, in Your mercy . . . hear our prayer.

Father of all love and compassion, we thank You for all the representatives from the various charities who came to share with us the work they do for the poor and the vulnerable. We support them in prayer this morning and ask You to give these organisations extraordinary abilities and protection for their much-valued work. Grant us all a caring and loving heart for all those in need, near or far . . . including our enemies.

Lord, in You mercy . . . hear our prayer.

Lord, we pray for the recipients of the help, sent to them by the generosity of many. Fill their hearts with gratitude. God of abundance, we pray that You would multiply and protect what little these people have.

Lord, in Your mercy . . . hear our prayer.

Lord, we pray that during this prayer time may, through Your Holy Word, You speak to each one of us. Grant us a listening heart, I beg.

Pause . . .

If you help the poor, you are lending to the Lord, and God will repay you.

Pause . . .

Those who oppress the poor insult their Maker. But he who shows compassion and mercy towards the needy, honour the Lord.

Long pause . . .

Holy Spirit, we thank You for speaking to us through Your Word. Amen.

Intercessory Prayer No: 7

The theme of our prayer is the Second Coming of Jesus:

Lord Jesus Christ said, 'The Son of Man is going to come in His Father's glory with His angels, and then He will reward each person according to what he or she has done.'

- Father God, You have proved to us that You are true and faithful to Your promises. We praise You that all the prophecies concerning the First Coming of Jesus were fulfilled precisely as the prophets said. This gives us the guarantee that the Lord Jesus Christ is definitely coming back to this earth again, as promised. Lord, please help us to hold on to all the promises concerning the Second Coming of Jesus. May we share this good news with others that Jesus, the God Almighty, is coming to make everything new, and may we also encourage others to be prepared for His arrival.

The Church and the Spirit say: Come, Lord Jesus. Come quickly.

- Lord Jesus Christ, You promised that You are going to heaven to prepare a place and then come back to take us there. So Lord, help Your Church to keep herself pure and ready when You come to take us with You.

The Church and the Spirit say: Come, Lord Jesus. Come quickly.

- We call upon You, Lord Jesus Christ, to come quickly. Come and deliver us from the corrupted world we live in. Lord Jesus Christ, come and establish Your everlasting kingdom on earth with Your light, life, love, peace, justice, power, and righteousness.

The Church and the Spirit say: Come, Lord Jesus. Come quickly.

- Lord Jesus Christ, the Judge of all nations, please come with Your angels from Your throne of glory and decide the future of each nation so that peace, love, justice, and harmony prevail in the world.

The Church and the Spirit say: Come, Lord Jesus. Come quickly.

- Lord Jesus Christ, come and vindicate that You are God, the glorious risen Saviour, the Judge, and the King of the universe, as every eye is going to behold You descending from heaven. But we do offer our prayers to soften the hearts of those who hate, ignore, and reject You, before it is too late.

The Church and the Spirit say: Come, Lord Jesus. Come quickly.

- Lord Jesus Christ, we are longing for that day when You will come again to completely destroy Satan, sin, and death, and then there will be no more sickness or pain, no presence of sin and Satan, and no more death. But in the meantime, please help us to watch and pray through Your Word and to be obedient to Your commands.

The Church and the Spirit say: Come, Lord Jesus. Come quickly.

- Lord Jesus Christ, we thank You and praise You that You are coming again to share Your glory with the people who are redeemed by Your blood. Lord, help us to share this good news with others so that many more will share the hope of glory in the Lord Jesus Christ.

The Church and the Spirit say: Come, Lord Jesus. Come quickly.

Lord, accept these prayers for the sake of Your Son Jesus Christ. Amen.

Chapter 5

The Conclusive Prayer

Praying through Psalm 23

Lord Jesus Christ, accept my sacrifice of praise and thanks for being my good, loving, and perfect Shepherd.

Jesus, You are the Shepherd who is super rich in all resources because you own everything in heaven and on this earth. Therefore, You are sufficient for my physical, emotional, mental, social, and spiritual needs.

Oh Divine Shepherd, how can I follow another shepherd when you have restored my soul with Your love, with Your life, and with Your power? You are my wisdom, my courage, and my strength.

I thank and praise You that You daily lead me, guide me, and protect me along the right paths. Let these daily provisions for me give You immense pleasure, and bring honour and glory to Your holy name.

Oh Victorious Shepherd, I worship and praise You for giving Your life on the Cross and conquering Satan, sin, and death. So I put my trust in You, for You have the power and the authority to lead me safely through the passages of trial, darkness, and death. I will not be afraid of any other influence or any other power that can intimidate me.

Lord, I am confident of this that the love, mercy, and goodness of my Shepherd will always be available to me all the days of my life on this earth, and I will spend all eternity in Your presence. Amen.

H. R. Chowdhry

Do you need Prayer Support?

1. Contact Lifeline:
   Premier Lifeline is a confidential telephone helpline offering a listening ear along with emotional and spiritual support from a Christian perspective and prayer.

   Lifeline telephone numbers:
   0845 345 0707 (BT Local Rate)
   020 7316 0808
   Premier Lifeline is open 9am to midnight everyday of the year.
   www.premier.org.uk

2. Contact Prayerline:
   UCB Prayerline is all about bringing God into the equation of your life. This confidential service is available to you whoever you are and whatever background you come from. Whatever the issues you are facing, trained Christian volunteers will take your call and pray for you and with you.

   Prayerline telephone numbers:
   0845 456 7729(UK)
   1890 940 300 (ROI)
   ucb.co.uk